HESTON
BLUMENTHAL

HESTON
BLUMENTHAL

THE BIOGRAPHY OF THE WORLD'S MOST BRILLIANT MASTER CHEF

CHAS NEWKEY-BURDEN

JOHN BLAKE

Published by John Blake Publishing Ltd,
3 Bramber Court, 2 Bramber Road,
London W14 9PB, England

www.johnblakepublishing.co.uk

www.facebook.com/Johnblakepub   facebook

twitter.com/johnblakepub   twitter

First published in hardback in 2009.
This edition published in paperback in 2012.

ISBN: 978-1-84358-956-3

British Library Cataloguing-in-Publication Data:

A catalogue record for this book is available from the British Library.

Design by www.envydesign.co.uk

Printed and bound by CPI Group (UK) Ltd, Croydon, CR0 4YY

1 3 5 7 9 10 8 6 4 2

Papers used by John Blake Publishing are natural, recyclable products made
from wood grown in sustainable forests. The manufacturing processes
conform to the environmental regulations of the country of origin.

Every attempt has been made to contact the relevant copyright-holders,
but some were unobtainable. We would be grateful if the
appropriate people could contact us.

CONTENTS

PROLOGUE

It was, for Heston Blumenthal, a 'eureka' moment...

As he learned the art of cooking, he loved to read books about the culinary world. They fired his imagination and fuelled his ambition. He would spend hours poring over their words and pictures, learning the tricks of the trade. The lives of the chefs depicted in their pages seemed to him to be extraordinarily glamorous. These almost mythical men combined a working life of cooking and experimenting in the kitchen with a decadent leisure lifestyle in such exotic locations as the south of France. He would build his own library of cooking-related books, not just straightforward recipe titles, though there would be plenty of them. When he got older he would also read tomes about the principles behind food and its preparation, but the book that first captured his imagination was called *On Food and Cooking: The Science and Lore of the Kitchen* and he came across this when he was 19 years old. Written by American food guru Harold McGee, the book was bursting with knowledge and enthusiasm for the art of cookery. Heston bought it the year it was first published – 1986 – and found that, in every sense, it spoke his language. Here was a scientific approach to food and cooking, although that was initially secondary to his connection with McGee's manifesto. It was when Heston turned to page 115 of the book that his heart really raced and his mind truly became enlivened. McGee wrote that, contrary to wisdom accepted since the middle of the 19th century, searing a meat does not seal it. This might not seem significant to the layman, but to the cooking world this was a revolutionary pronouncement. The entire culinary world had believed without question that searing sealed a meat, effectively creating a shell around it. Yet here was McGee trampling all over that received wisdom.

Blumenthal's mind was blown by this news. For years, he had pursued a scientific approach to food, an approach that McGee swore by too. However, the realisation that the unquestionable truth was *not* actually true prompted Blumenthal to fundamentally change his approach towards cuisine. It was not the detail of searing that made such an impact, more what the principle could mean for the rest of cooking. A list of other written-in-stone cooking principles flashed through his mind. How many of them might be on closer, clear-minded inspection open to serious debate too?

He thought and began to wonder whether the accepted approach for so many principles and ideas of cooking had held back his predecessors. How much higher could he rise, now that he had adopted a very basic, but utterly fundamental principle which would be summed up in two words: *question everything*.

INTRODUCTION

Heston Blumenthal is a master of combining contrasting flavours in his dishes to wonderful effect. Indeed, his entire approach is ruled by a pleasing paradox: he is an eccentric with a love of dishes that are named as if they have lofty pretensions, yet, amid his tireless experimentation and use of expensive ingredients, he always retains the common touch. As he pointed out in his book *In Search of Perfection*, 'For many of us, the perfect meal won't be some fancy restaurant food.' He goes on to explain that the desert island dish most people would nominate would be something homely. Likewise, the dishes most requested as a last meal by the condemned men of death row are usually things such as burger and fries, egg and bacon or ice cream – everyday dishes, rather than gastronomic luxuries or complex-tasting menus. When we look at some of Blumenthal's most outlandish dishes – bacon and egg ice cream, snail porridge and the like – we see that he is combining gastronomic excellence with just these sorts of familiar comfort-food bases.

Indeed, given the theatre with which he serves many of his dishes – iPods playing the sounds of the sea are provided alongside a seafood dish, cakes have 'orgasms' on the plate by firing out white chocolate mousse when the diner cuts in – it is clear that Blumenthal is not only aiming his food at those for whom a £100+ meal is an everyday norm. Rather, his target audience include those among us who have to save up for a really special treat and want to savour every moment and mouthful. Blumenthal understands these people because back in his twenties he was one of them. Indeed, despite being financially far better off these days, he remains one of them.

Away from his working life, Heston Blumenthal enjoys the simple foods of the world as much as he does the more extravagant ones. Although he finds it hard to eat regularly with his family due to the immense demands of his job, when he does, he insists that they eat down-to-earth grub.

Each Sunday at 5pm, the family sit down to a traditional Sunday roast and on Monday evening it is always a curry, often ordered in from his local takeaway. When he wants to eat out, it is far from unheard of to see him at a Pizza Express restaurant or even queuing up at the doner kebab van in Marlow, the Berkshire town where he lives. 'There's nothing wrong with kebab,' he says, 'apart from the fat it contains.' With the occasional exception, he sees his indulgences not at the table, but in the kitchen. 'My biggest indulgence is work,' he says.

But this ordinary home life should not detract at all from the magical results of Blumenthal's hours of work and experimentation in his development kitchen in Bray. The very names of his dishes are dazzling enough – to eat them is always a multi-sensory, unforgettable experience. Seemingly without any effort, he gives the impression that there is no end to his abilities. As one journalist wrote of Blumenthal, 'He could probably make you a cloud sandwich if you asked. Or a blancmange made of numbers. He can do anything, basically.'

To the casual observer, he might seem like a vision from futuristic culinary fantasy, but there is only once place that Blumenthal would journey to if he were given a time-travel machine: the past. To say Blumenthal is a nostalgic man is something of an understatement. So much of his work involves him trying to recapture childhood memories. Food for him takes him back to a time of reassurance; smells, flavours and even the sound and appearance of food are for him strongly evocative.

All of this has led to Blumenthal being compared to numerous figures. A regular person that he is compared to is Willy Wonka, of Roald Dahl's classic for children *Charlie and the Chocolate Factory*. Wonka is a genius recluse and eccentric character who runs a magical chocolate factory which makes exciting treats such as Everlasting Gobstoppers and Whipple-Scrumptious Fudgemallow Delight.

However, as we shall see, the childhood novel that most speaks to him is Lewis Carroll's *Alice in Wonderland*, a story he frequently alludes to. There is indeed something of the childhood scientist about the way he goes about his experimentation. Here is evidence of a man who is truly joyful in his work. For where do any of us go in our minds when we are happiest but to our childhood?

Blumenthal is a man who is at play as he works. What an enviable position to be in! Even when he explains why he crops his hair, he takes the conversation back several decades. 'Have you seen the *Hair Bear Bunch* from the 1970s?' he asks. 'The truth is I have the biggest mop of red hair; it's like strapping a doormat to my head. I could have a ginger afro – the truth is out!'

He is a humble man despite his enormous success and fame. When he went to Buckingham Palace to receive an OBE from the Queen in 2006, he was standing next to fashion designer Ozwald Boateng, who was also about to be gonged. Blumenthal regarded those alongside them, including those devoted to their community and people who had worked on behalf of ethnic minorities. He turned to the fashion designer and said, 'There are all these people who've done amazing charity work and then there's me who's getting a gong for chopping a few onions and you who's getting one for a bit of sewing.'

He wasn't convinced Boateng appreciated the point, but nonetheless the comment shows how Blumenthal remains a modest man. Not that he is playing down the significance of his honour. 'Don't get me wrong,' he added. 'I'm not giving my OBE up for anyone. That was one of the proudest moments of my life. What I was really saying was that we were there for doing something self-indulgent, something we love doing. I felt a lack of worthiness at the time. But I've got it and I'm not giving it back!'

Again, we return to the joy of Blumenthal's work. The stereotype that those who cook are often sad people does not apply here. 'Dining should be a thing of pleasure, enrichment and stimulation. It should excite, charm and challenge, but above all it should be fun,' he has said, adding with boyish enthusiasm and one of those nods to *Alice* that he considers his work to be akin to 'popping down the rabbit-hole of culinary history'.

And yet, despite his common touch, Blumenthal would not deny that the way he goes about his work is frequently very fussy and outlandish. He feels that all his complicated efforts are always sensible and justified, however. 'Sometimes people have suggested to me that life's too short for the kind of lengths to which I go to create a recipe. But if it results in something delicious, stimulating and surprising, if it turns a meal into an event, a piece of real pleasure, then surely it's worth it?'

It's hard to argue with him. In the final analysis, he lives by the maxim of American chef Julia Child, who says: 'Non-cooks think it's silly to invest two hours' work in two minutes' enjoyment; but, if cooking is evanescent, well, so is the ballet.'

There are, of course, limits to the eccentricity he would introduce at The Fat Duck. He recalled, for instance, a sanitary lesson he learned during an encounter in Holland. 'This scientist wanted to demonstrate how saliva bonds to fat and protein molecules, so he gave me a spoonful of custard then, when I'd swallowed it, stuck a tampon in my mouth for a while. Then I had a second spoonful of custard and it tasted much richer. It's all about how you can make custard seem more creamy with a dry mouth. It's interesting stuff, but I'm not going to start serving Fat Duck customers with Tampax before they eat.' A very wise decision, though one suspects that, if anyone could pull off a tampon with their dish, Blumenthal would be the man.

His ascent has come during an era of culinary renaissance in Britain. As our media has both reflected and driven our increased interest in food, the standing of the chef has risen in public esteem. However, this forms another interesting paradox: as the rise of ready-meals, takeaways and the microwave ovens amid increasingly hectic lifestyles mean that we the public cook less proper meals, so does our interest in famous chefs rise. There is an aspirational dimension to this: as a character in Monica Ali's novel *In the Kitchen* says, the less we cook, the more we want to watch them cook instead. They have become like rock stars or movie actors.

Jamie Oliver, Gordon Ramsay, Raymond Blanc, Ainsley Harriott and Hugh Fearnley-Whittingstall form the premier league in the crowded genre of the professional chef, where they are joined by a resurgent Delia Smith. It was an area of standing room only but Blumenthal brought something new with his geeky, boyish ways. Where he fits in among them can best be seen by the egg. Delia Smith showed us how to boil an egg on television, Ainsley Harriott would dance around it, Jamie Oliver would preach about it and Gordon

Ramsay would swear at it. Blumenthal, meanwhile, showed us how to use it to make liquid nitrogen-cooked egg and bacon ice cream.

He loves his work and that is, ultimately, his charm and his fortune. Since opening The Fat Duck restaurant he has been full of enthusiasm for his profession. 'I've only once got into the car in the morning thinking, I don't wanna go to work, and I think that's a really lucky thing,' he has said. In summing himself up, he conjures up another contrast: 'I'm a geezer with a childlike inquisitiveness.'

He is the world's most brilliant master chef. Here is his story.

CHAPTER ONE
THE KARATE KID

To paraphrase an old football billboard advertisement, 1966 was an eventful year for England: the national football team won the World Cup, Harold Wilson's Labour Party won the general election, The Beatles released their acclaimed album *Revolver* – celebrating the release by declaring themselves 'bigger than Jesus' – the Kray twins shot a rival; and, on 27 May, Heston Blumenthal was born in West London. (Blumenthal is not the only British celebrity chef to arrive on this date, a certain Jamie Oliver was born on the same day, just nine years later.)

Blumenthal grew up in the Shepherds Bush district of West London with his parents Stephen and Celia and his sister. This is not a part of the world hugely associated with cuisine and dining. True, it has its fair share of restaurants but the leisure activities most associated with Shepherds Bush are football, theatre, live music and television. The local team, Queens Park Rangers, play their home games at nearby

Loftus Road. (Blumenthal himself is a confirmed Arsenal fan, visiting the Emirates Stadium a couple of times a season. He once went into business with a Gunners' legend.)

Venues such as the Bush Theatre put on great plays and concerts, the Shepherds Bush Empire is a hot live music venue and the BBC has many offices and studios in the area. Therefore, it is more likely that the celebrity side of Blumenthal, rather than the chef side, was awakened by his experiences growing up in Shepherds Bush.

But, as far as food is concerned, there has long been a South African flavour to the area. Some street names in Shepherds Bush hark towards the country, and the area used to be home to a venue called the South African Pavilion. Nowadays, the distinctive accent of the region can be heard in the area, as part of the general influx of its inhabitants into West London.

Although Heston Blumenthal's father, Stephen, had an English background, he was born in Zimbabwe and raised in South Africa. The family returned to England as apartheid began to cause increasing conflict, but they would still holiday in South Africa when Blumenthal was growing up. There were some early food experiences for him on those trips, such as the meaty delights of *boerewors* (spicy sausages) and tasty, juicy steaks. He was fascinated by the flavours and textures of these foods.

It is only natural to look for clues in the early years of someone for the person they became. However, for Blumenthal, being a cook was not an ambition that he forged particularly early in life. Instead, he originally wanted to be an inventor. This stemmed from a story he wrote at school at the age of seven. 'I wrote a story about a spaceship that could go anywhere in the universe, even to Ireland,' he remembered. As far as the Emerald Isle? That's some spaceship, Heston. However, his ambition to become an inventor has not gone entirely unrealised, for Heston has been at the cutting edge of cooking, rather than one who follows either the pack or the rules. So it can be said that he realised his ambition, but in the kitchen rather than in hops across the Irish sea in a spaceship. Well, it's not a bad second prize, is it?

Not that he is lacking in memories of food as a kid, as we have already seen. Blumenthal is now a famous chef, not least due to the numerous television programmes he has presented. He was inspired from an early age to combine food and broadcasting when his imagination was captured by one of the earliest cooking personalities, Graham Kerr.

Born in 1934, Kerr was one of the earliest celebrity chefs in the UK, although his profile was first raised as a result of a trip to New Zealand. He emigrated down under in 1958 to work as a culinary consultant to the armed forces. One day, he appeared on television to demonstrate how to cook an omelette. He charmed the viewers and he was soon offered a regular spot on Australian television. He also contributed recipes to the pages of glossy magazines and published his own book – *Entertaining With Kerr*.

Then, in 1969, Kerr moved to Canada where he presented a show called *The Galloping Gourmet*. It was named after a book he co-authored with wine bod Len Evans, based on a jolly jaunt the pair made across the globe. However, in the television show of the same name, it really was all about Kerr. He would leap around the set, crack jokes and neck gulps of wine as he cooked. More than anything else, the programme is perhaps best remembered for the fact that Kerr used large amounts of butter, cream and other high-cholesterol ingredients. He was devil-may-care and often said to his guests of these fattening factors, 'Madame, you could go outside and get run over by a bus and just think what you would have missed!' It was all good fun and *The Galloping Gourmet* earned himself two Emmy nominations in the process, as well as young Heston Blumenthal's continued admiration.

Two events in Kerr's life radically changed his outlook. Firstly, in 1971, he was involved in a serious car crash that left him paralysed for a while. Then his wife suffered a stroke and a heart attack. The Kerr that returned to the television screens after these setbacks was a changed man. More serious than the carefree cook of before, he would include a quote from the Bible as part of his shows. And the high-fat recipes were history as well. Instead, he produced dishes which he dubbed Minimax – the name formed from 'minimum' amount of fat and the 'maximum' amount of flavour and texture. Kerr's shows grabbed the attention of Blumenthal as he grew up watching television in the family home in West London, in the shadows of the BBC headquarters. One of his earliest memories of watching the box was of Kerr 'standing back as he shook a flaming pan while the audience cheered'.

There was also plenty of cooking at home. Heston's mother has always cooked a great coq au vin, and many of his childhood food memories revolve around the Christian festive season. Heston considers himself Jewish, yet agnostic. He has always celebrated Christmas, for instance. 'Childhood memories are key to my cooking,' he has said. 'And, of course, many of the most vivid childhood memories are of Christmas.' It is a season full of scents and smells, particularly for the ultra-sensorially aware Blumenthal, who would later draw upon them as inspiration for a flaming sorbet dish. 'When I was a kid, we used to go to my uncle's house in London. I remember being cold and walking into his warm house as he had a big open log fire. The heat and light and the crackling sound of the fire mixed with the smell of his oak-panelled room, his tobacco and the whisky by his leather chair always bring Christmases of my childhood strongly to my thoughts.'

As we will see, he had a wake-up call one Christmas as an adult, which made him determined to try harder on his relationship with his own children. He says that the key to a good Christmas dinner is 'organisation and to remember you are not just doing it for other people but for yourself as well. You've got to enjoy it or there's no point. And cut down on the number of dishes you serve. Do fewer things well.' Of his nightmare Christmas guests, he says they would be vegans. 'I completely understand vegetarianism, and there are some wonderful pleasures in eating food that doesn't involve meat and fish. But Christmas is an occasion when people come together friends, family for social interaction around the table, and when you decide you're not going to eat the meat or fish, then surely you get no enjoyment from that, and, well, I just think you shouldn't be there.'

His mother's favourite dishes included warming fare such as Hungarian goulash and Coronation chicken. Heston's first memory of cooking himself was when he camped in the back garden of the family home and cooked a sausage over a fire. He burned it but was proud of his first cooking experience. *He* had cooked it, he explains, so to *him* it tasted marvellous. A burned sausage is not something that is likely to appear on the tasting menu of The Fat Duck any time soon, but he did return to the open-air cooking of sausages on his BBC television programme *In Search of Perfection* in later years.

Two culinary childhood memories that are firmly implanted in Heston's mind are being ticked off royally for breaking the seal on a pressure cooker that was boiling some chicken broth. The floor in their flat was uneven and, when the young Heston jumped up and down as his mother was cooking yet another dish in the pressure cooker, the vibrations could cause the valve of the cooker to fly off. This would be immediately followed by a blast of escaping steam, much to his excitement.

A more harmonious memory is that of his impatience waiting to be able to eat newly prepared cheesecake. It took a day for the cake to set and Heston would become extremely enthusiastic at the prospect and impatient to eat it. He also remembers sometimes seeing an avocado pear in the fridge, an exotic ingredient for a home in that decade. How things have changed: nowadays an avocado pear would be one of the least surprising items in a Blumenthal kitchen.

He is keen to not overplay the part that the preparation of food played in his early years. 'Although my mother was a very good cook, my childhood memories were not woven with gastronomic experiences,' he insisted. 'I didn't spend hours beside her, stoning cherries or peeling potatoes. Food nostalgia for my generation was quite heavily influenced by synthetic flavours such as strawberry Angel Delight.' Not that he was a fan of Angel Delight alone. Indeed, the treat he truly delighted in appears to have been ice cream.

'When I was young we went to Par Sands in Cornwall,' he recalled in the *Guardian*. It was a culinary experience in a whole range of ways. 'My old man used olive oil as suntan lotion; we'd eat Shippam's meat-paste sandwiches and ice cream for pudding. It was always a fight to eat the ice cream, licking the top so it didn't fall all over your fingers, sucking the remainder out of the bottom. I remember picnics by the coast, with floral tables that collapsed as we battled the elements. Through it all, ice cream was our beacon of hope.' A sweet-tasting lighthouse, perhaps. This was the 1970s and so the ice cream range was not as exotic as it is today. 'Back then, of course, it was either Neapolitan ice cream or these nuclear orange blocks wrapped in cardboard,' he recalled. There was none of your Ben & Jerry's and Häagen-Dazs back then.

But it was not just his father who shaped Heston's love of ice cream and nor was Cornwall the only place he ate it. Back in West London, he would partake of it with some gusto.

'Every Saturday morning, my grandmother would take my sister and I to her favourite haunt: Church Street market, off Edgware Road,' he told the *Guardian*. For the young Heston, traipsing round the antique and junk stores was hard work. However, there was always a treat at the end to make up for it. 'On the way back, my grandmother would treat the pair of us to a tub of vanilla ice cream ... Just the thought of the contents of that carton made the couple of minutes that it took to walk home before devouring it seem like an age.' The shop they bought the ice creams from was called the Regent Snack Bar, run by a family from Sicily. It had a pistachio-green interior and a symbolic ice cream cone above its entry.

Blumenthal vividly recalls that a man dressed in a white coat would fill the ice cream orders. Heston's favourite order was vanilla ice cream with a hint of coffee. He always imagined that this combination was achieved by simply mixing a tiny amount of coffee into a vanilla base. However, as he began to experiment later in life in the hope of reproducing this childhood favourite, he found he could not get it right. So he tracked down the man in the white coat, now working in Chiswick, and discovered that the method was a lot less subtle than that. The man simply combined 50 per cent vanilla ice cream and 50 per cent coffee ice cream. All the same, an ice cream fan had been born.

Blumenthal still remembers hearing the tune of the ice-cream van and the hurried process that followed to make sure they were out on the street with their money in time to buy a 99 complete with chocolate flake before the van motored off to its next stopping point. Evocative stuff, and

Heston to this day associates the tinkle of the ice cream van with summer alongside other memories such as wasps and lawnmowers. He also ate ice cream at the local cinema he attended regularly on Saturday mornings where he would enjoy a tub during the interval midway through that week's choice of movie. Who could have guessed then what headline-grabbing innovations he would bring to ice cream – among many other foods – in later years?

On long trips across the country, the family would sometimes stop at motorway service stations. There, he first experienced the joys of Little Chef restaurants that were to become such a famous part of his career many decades on. As a kid, he loved the entire Little Chef experience. 'You could get fishfingers … in the actual shape of fish,' he recalled. 'Bliss. And the traffic-light lollipop with which they sent you on your way was the crowning glory of many a 1970s childhood.' These vivid memories and the warmth with which they are delivered show just how much of an impact, and a positive one at that, Little Chef had on him.

His family also sometimes ate at the Berni Inn chain. Founded in 1955 as a one-off in Bristol, it soon opened branches across the country. There, discerning diners were introduced to the wonders of steak dishes, prawn cocktails and Black Forest Gateau. 'You're better off at Berni,' ran the advertising slogan. 'We're famous for our steaks,' said another. The chain soon became something of a joke, particularly among food snobs. TV comedy character Alan Partridge once asked a fictional French chef guest on his show, 'Now, you are known as the top chef in your field.

You've only got one restaurant; Berni Inn has thousands: jealous?' Straight-talking chef Gordon Ramsay remembers visiting a Berni Inn restaurant in the early 1980s. He summed it up in one word: 'Hideous'.

Blumenthal also recalls sampling steaks at the home of a Portuguese friend – although the most memorable part of the sampling was through his nose. His friend's mother would often fry steaks, and the smell that emanated from the kitchen always captured Heston's imagination. He describes it as akin to the scenes from those classic television advertisements for Bisto gravy, in which the cartoon children hold their noses up high to savour the distinctive odour of the brand.

No Berni Inn restaurant experience back then was complete without a Black Forest Gateau, but Heston would try to pick off just the chocolate part, as he found the gateau experience in its entirety a considerable letdown. He still wonders whether anyone really enjoyed them and later set out to investigate the dish as an adult.

Only on special occasions would the Blumenthal clan normally venture elsewhere. For instance, they would sometimes have picnics in Windsor Great Park, in the shadow of the magnificent castle. A 5,000-acre affair that dates from the 13th century, it is a popular attraction for the people not only from Berkshire – where Blumenthal would later live and work – but also from West London and beyond.

In addition to the al fresco Windsor treats, every year on his birthday, Heston's parents would take him to eat out. They would normally go to the Lee Ho Fook Chinese restaurant on Queensway, West London. Young Heston was always excited by these visits and basked in the sensory overload of the restaurant's exotic cooking smells, the sight of the prepared ducks hanging in the window and, of course, the challenge of eating with chopsticks. It was an exciting experience for a kid in the 1970s when such Eastern wonders were still a rarity. Indeed, when his friends came for dinner, Heston would worry that their pallets would be unable to cope with dishes as out of the ordinary as the Coronation chicken and goulash that his mother served them. She sometimes cooked spaghetti Bolognese, too. He recalls that she believed – as did most people back then – that Bolognese sauce was in essence no different to that of shepherd's pie or chilli con carne. He would find mushrooms and peas in his mother's version of the former. These were simple times for most domestic kitchens.

Another birthday experience for young Heston came at a fish and chips restaurant. Norfolk Place, near Paddington Station, housed a fine such establishment back then called Micky's Fish Bar, which remains open to this day. Heston's father sometimes called in on his journey home from work and picked up food for the family. They would douse them in Sarson's vinegar and eat them straight from the paper they had been wrapped in. Heston would burrow down to the bottom of the paper to find any last bits of fish, batter and chips that might have been hidden in a corner. One year, on his birthday, Heston's father allowed him to go in and order the food himself. He was mesmerised by the noises, colours and smells of Micky's Fish Bar. Again, this was a childhood memory he returned to professionally later in life, when he sought to perfect the dish on his BBC television series.

He recalls that British restaurants in this era were unimaginative. London's eateries focused on safe-bet dishes like chicken kiev and duck a l'orange. The restaurants' interiors were often on the gaudy side, with flock wallpaper a feature of not just Indian restaurants but of all nationalities. No wonder, he argues, that restaurant scenes soon became a rich mine of comedy for British sitcom writers.

Throughout the 1970s, comedy was often to be found in scenes of uncomfortable meals shared in dowdy restaurants. Heston loved these sorts of classic British comedy shows, and still does to this day, for their accurate portrayal of the gastronomic scene in England in that period. As he points out, one of the more imaginative creations of the restaurant scene in the 1970s was the 'chicken in a basket' – a dish thought to have originated in a Cotswolds pub in the 1960s, in which a chicken would be served on a bed of fried chips in a wicker basket. Another favourite for the teenage Heston was the pizza. With typically adolescent fervour, he used to load them with as many toppings as possible, everything from artichokes to pepperoni. He would sometimes eat pizzas at his local cinema as he watched films, though he was not over impressed by the dense, smelly fare served up by most pizzerias of the period.

Early culinary attempts by Blumenthal himself, back home in his own kitchen, were imaginative enough for a young lad. One day he attempted to make the ultimate sandwich, containing every favourite ingredient of his: jelly, jam, Nutella and peanut butter spreads and hundreds-and-thousands. The result was interesting, presumably sending the youngster into a sugar rush of immense proportions, followed by a considerable crash.

In a rather psychological interview later in life, Heston spoke somewhat sombrely about his formative years, saying that, of late, he had 'started thinking a lot more about my upbringing which on the surface was a great childhood. But it's amazing how your actions – even when you think they're fine – can be subconsciously damaging.'

But he was physically active as a youngster, taking up karate and kick-boxing. Soon he was practising these martial arts for up to ten hours and began to enter competitions across the UK. This was no passing fancy, it was a pastime he took very seriously and into which he threw his enormous ambition, energy and discipline. Here was a way to channel his energy and anger as a teenager. He thrashed around on the mats and something about the experience spoke to him – it was a mixture of adrenalin and discipline, focus and aggression. It was a noble art and one at which he did fairly well.

He took his classes in Buckinghamshire where the family had by this stage moved. 'There were a load of Wycombe hard-nuts down there, potentially quite dangerous people, but I was the youngest person and the moment they saw I wanted to learn they took me under their wing and it was a really great feeling of camaraderie,' he recalls fondly. However, as he reached the middle of his teenage years, his back problems were becoming increasingly serious. 'By the time I was 15, I was having regular sessions with an osteopath to try to resolve the problem,' he remembered. The metal plate that had been inserted into his back was not all bad news. When he filmed a television show for the BBC, it meant he could justifiably ask someone else to perform a difficult task, as we shall see.

Meanwhile, at school, Heston was a studious and hardworking boy. He was attending the John Hampden Grammar School in High Wycombe. Based in Marlow Hill, opposite a sports centre, it is a boys' school with a fine reputation. He also spent time at Latymer Upper School in Hammersmith, West London, another well-renowned school, which includes model Lily Cole, comedian Mel Smith and actor Hugh Grant among its alumni.

Blumenthal would happily work hard on a Friday evening getting his homework done, and his focus was rewarded: he got six O-Level passes. Then he joined the sixth form and became rather distracted, resulting in just the one A-Level pass – in art. Even that pass came, he said, as a result of 'fortuitous revision the night before'. But he was intrigued by the paintings *Ascending and Descending* and *Belvedere* by Dutch artist MC Escher.

He was not a young man lacking in curiosity, as we shall see. However, he did not go on to university and nor was he encouraged to by his parents. His father, who studied architecture and did a furniture-restoration course, put no pressure on him. Looking back, Heston now feels that he would have liked to study psychology or history. In fact, he maintains an interest in psychology to this day, but, for all his interest in history, a family holiday was about to give Blumenthal something to get excited about in his *future*...

CHAPTER TWO

I WAS GOING TO SMACK HIM ONE

It was to be a family holiday that changed 16-year-old Heston Blumenthal's life. The year was 1982 and the destination was France. His father was doing well in his business so the family travelled across the sea for a special holiday which would include an epochal experience for their son. The Blumenthals had lunch at a Provençal three-star restaurant called L'Oustau de Baumaniere.

'That was it,' he recalled. 'Gastronomy was for me.' L'Oustau de Baumaniere was fun and stylish. He has since described eating there and his experience as akin to love at first sight. He certainly recalls the details of that visit with the sort of precision that people recall meeting the love of their life for the first time. Afternoon was blending into evening as the family car took the snaking path to the restaurant. No wonder, thought young Blumenthal, that it was named after the underworld – a literal translation of the area's name, Val d'Enfer, being 'valley of hell'. The cliffs and caves gave it a rather purgatorial edge. They parked and Blumenthal noted the surroundings once more. He had the feeling he was about to experience something new and unique.

They ate outside and he found the experience to be akin to theatre, with both the staff and the diners key players in the drama. He remembers the moustache of the restaurant owner, the smell of the lavender in the air and the presence of a helipad. It was all worlds apart from a West London Berni Inn!

The restaurant was run by a man called Raymond Thuilier. Born in Chambery, Savoie, on 11 January 1897, Thuilier, the chef and owner of the restaurant, was a colourful character, who revolutionised French cuisine in the 20th century. Thuilier's father died when he was just three years old and the boy grew up watching his mother cook at a restaurant. When he grew up, he served in the army and then turned to insurance sales. Having made a decent packet through the latter pursuit, in 1941, he bought a ruined farmhouse in the French village of Les Baux. He spent five years lovingly restoring the property to its former glory and then paved the floor. The seats were adorned with Gobelin tapestry. In 1954, he won three Michelin stars.

He died at the age of 96 in the summer of 1993. As his obituary in the *Independent* newspaper said, 'As a cook, Raymond Thuilier was firmly of the school of Point: a completely clean kitchen and fine, fresh ingredients every day, from identifiable and dependable sources. Apart from these basic tenets, he had no truck with the nouvelle cuisine of the 1970s and 1980s.' For instance, when the Queen visited in 1972, he served her a sea bass en croute with a prawn sauce and a baron of lamb.

He also believed firmly in the importance of the surroundings in which a meal was consumed. 'It is not only what is on the plate that matters,' Thuilier said in 1990. 'It is the environment, the welcome. A grand Bordeaux in a bad glass is no longer a grand Bordeaux.' This element of his approach is one that Blumenthal passionately subscribes to.

Thuilier was a charismatic man. An American journalist described him as a 'jovial, mustachioed Frenchman who looked as if he'd just heard some good news about himself'. One day, a diner at his restaurant complained that his green beans were not fresh enough. On hearing this news, Thuilier was furious. He stormed off and then returned to the table with a huge box of beans which he threw over the diner's table. 'Get out of my restaurant and don't ever come here again,' he screamed at the aghast guest. It's hard to imagine Blumenthal ever responding to criticism in such a way, despite his well-publicised issues with anger and the words of one of his Fat Duck waiters who said he wouldn't want to get on the wrong side of his boss.

Having dined at Thuilier's famous restaurant, Heston's life was changed forever. He was enthused by the experience and developed an obsession with food. He bought the *Michelin Guide* and the *GaultMillau*, two revered books of the world that Thuilier lived in. Now, back home in England, Heston could recall his experience at Les Baux and dream of more time in that world.

The *Michelin Guide* holds an almost biblical authority over restaurants. Put together from the reports of full-time expert inspectors who anonymously visit restaurants, it is a work of obsession for the benefit of those dedicated to the pursuit of fine dining. Restaurants would be judged on five main criteria: the quality of the products; the mastery of flavour and cooking; the 'personality' of the cuisine; value for money; and consistency between visits. This last criterion is key to the Michelin experience. If inspectors were impressed by a restaurant, they would revisit many times to see if the establishment was able to maintain the standards.

Within the pages of the *Guide* over which Heston lovingly pored, restaurants were judged and assessed using a series of symbols that have become legendary in the industry. The fork and knives symbol ranges from one to five marks depending on quality of food; then there are the grapes to represent wine and a red or black symbol which indicates whether or not the restaurant has a view.

The *Michelin Guide* had a very different character to Heston's other main source of information at the time, the *GaultMillau*. First published in 1965, it had been founded by leading French restaurant critics Henri Gault and Christian Millau. And, although it was as authoritative as the *Michelin Guide*, it had more of an element of fun to it. Restaurants were assessed with marks out of 20 and they wouldn't even get to feature in the book unless they scored at least ten. Points were awarded purely on the quality of the food rather than other elements such as service, décor and so on. While the two founders were in control, no restaurant was ever awarded the full 20 marks. And yet, as Heston discovered, the book thought nothing of awarding a high score to a restaurant alongside a review of that restaurant that was extremely critical on many points. It's safe to say that the *GaultMillau*, for all its authority, did not take itself as seriously as the *Michelin Guide*. That said, its prose was more evocative. And back in England young Heston became obsessed with the two books and the world that they covered with such authority and expertise. He enjoyed comparing the way that the two publications would each review the same restaurant.

Nouvelle cuisine is, perhaps by definition, a term that has been redefined many times. In the 18th century, French chefs such as Vincent La Chapelle laid claim to it and, in the following century, Georges Auguste Escoffier was again credited with being responsible for a nouvelle cuisine. However, it was Gault and Millau who are most widely associated with the trend which was heralded by British magazine *Harpers & Queen* in 1975. Gone were the complications and large menus of previous chefs, and instead there was attention to detail, delicacy and a renewed focus on how food was presented to the diner.

Fresh food was the order of the day, with light flavourings and subtlety all round, in refreshing contrast to the rich and fattening food which had gone before. Not that it was an entirely French trend. It looked overseas for inspiration, with the Japanese styles of food presentation providing one key source of influence. The Californian health-conscious way of cooking was also to make its mark on the world of nouvelle cuisine. It was a modern, inventive, eclectic and experimental revolution. No wonder it so captured the imagination of the young Blumenthal.

As his love of the world of food increased, so did his appetite for the books that were published on the subject. When he discovered a new chef in the *Michelin Guide* or *GaultMillau*, he would obsessively research their work elsewhere. If they had a recipe book of their own, he had to have it; it was as simple as that. The cookery books transported him to a different world. The glamour, tastes and smells of the restaurants they described enchanted him, as did the drama and excitement of the venues themselves. The fact that he could have a little bit of that world in his own home, by studying these recipe books and trying their dishes out in his kitchen was very exciting. He collected books by chefs such as Alain Chapel, Fredy Girardet and Joël Robuchon, big-name French chefs, whose recipes he confidently attempted. He did not lack respect for them, but nor was he short of confidence as he embarked on this new passion.

He was particularly fond of the work of Alain Chapel, whose work was lauded by the *GaultMillau*: 'A meal at Chapel's restaurant was like a symphony.' Born in Lyon in 1937, Chapel learned the trade under his father who ran a bistro. The young man also spent time working in food stores, where he learned about different ingredients in detail. He also trained Fernand Point, often credited as the father of modern French cuisine, at his restaurant La Pyramide. Chapel then took over the family bistro and earned it its first Michelin star in 1967. Within seven years, he had three of them.

Heston studied the recipe book published by Chapel and made feverish notes in the margins of the pages. The book was in French and he would attempt to decipher Chapel's extravagant recipe instructions with the aid of a French-English dictionary. Heston's appetite for the written word is voracious. He rates *The Encyclopaedia of Practical Cookery* vols I and II, edited by Theodore Francis Garrett, as among his favourite culinary titles.

Blumenthal also enjoyed upmarket books with higher production values and glossiness than cookbooks. In his own high-quality tome *The Big Fat Duck Cookbook*, Heston recalls having read such publications as *Master Chefs of Europe*, *The Great Chefs of France* and *The Gourmet's Tour de France*. These books included sumptuous photographs of food and restaurants from the continental European streets. He particularly enjoyed the blow-by-blow descriptions of everyday life in restaurants.

The chefs, he discovered, would find all manner of fun ways to relax between their shifts. Some would go scuba diving, others would drive up and down the coastline of the south of France and some would turn to art. Their lifestyle seemed as romantic and tempting as he could imagine. Over and over he read these chapters, feeling more and more drawn to culinary elegance. The celebrity of these French stars appealed to him too. It seemed to be a joyful existence. These men were being paid not just to cook but to create, to innovate. In the process, they were enjoying playboy-style lives in France and becoming famous to boot. At first, it was more the trappings of their work that captured his imagination, rather than the intricacies of the cooking itself. He fancied a piece of that. Of course, being attracted to such a glamorous existence is hardly rare among teenage boys. He was so excited and could not wait to progress.

As soon as he turned 17, Blumenthal took driving lessons, like many young people, seeking the liberation and opportunities that having a car can bring. With Heston, there was a practical dimension as well as the general yearning for such freedom. With his own transport, he would be able to drive to faraway food stores and suppliers.

And so that was exactly what he did. Once he had passed his test, he would hop in his car and drive to wherever the best food could be bought. A particular favourite was a butcher's in Oxfordshire. There, he writes in *The Big Fat Duck Cookbook*, he would purchase a host of meat pieces to be taken straight home where they would become part of his latest concoction. Having spent weekday evenings reading about the recipes of his favourite chefs, he would hit the family kitchen at the weekend to try his hand at a few of the dishes.

He also developed a love of sherry in his twenties, and this too came during a trip to Oxfordshire. '[That was] where I also made my first and probably only great wine investment – a case of 1989 Chateau Le Pin for £330. Here I first tried a single Almacenista Amontillado from Lustau and realised sherry was something other than your aunt's tipple of choice, served in dodgy schooners at Christmas.' An enduring love was born there and then. 'I love sherry,' he has said since. 'There are so many to choose from, so I can't say I have a favourite, but at Christmas a Palo Cortado is fantastic. The process of making it is quite confusing, but it starts out as a different kind of sherry altogether: Amontillado. Then, for a slightly mysterious reason, a tiny amount of the Amontillado changes and develops into Palo Cortado. It's all about the yeasts in the juices.' He has since used sherry in some inventive ways.

Back then, Blumenthal would cook for the family whenever he could, because this meant his parents would fund his expenses for a meal. They were impressed with what their son served up, and 'hired' him to do the cooking for more than one of their own dinner parties. There, the friends of his parents would become the first members of the public to taste the food of Heston Blumenthal. Unlike diners at The Fat Duck, they did not have to hand over £130 for the privilege. Even at this tender age, Heston was not following the teenage clichés of knocking up a good spaghetti Bolognese for his parents to coo and clap over. No, Heston was already experimenting and innovating. When, during his weekday reading, he would get an idea for something unconventional to try, he was excited for the weekend when he could turn the family kitchen into a culinary laboratory. Heston has remained at great pains to describe himself as 'self-taught'. Well, it was in these hazy weekends of his late-teenage years that his education began in earnest. He worked hard and methodically.

To supplement the practical experimental lessons he

undertook at the weekend, he had all those weekday evenings that he spent studying. It was this that he drew upon as his primary source and he reflected upon what he had learned and drew conclusions. It was in every sense a course of education. That feverish last-minute revision which gained him his solitary A-Level was a thing of the past. Heston's studying of these books might have taken place in the evenings, but it was far from rushed and cursory. These books were becoming an obsession for him. It was just that the teacher and the student were both the same person: Heston Blumenthal. But he was soon to take a whole step up in his culinary education.

At the age of 18, Blumenthal began to look further than himself for his learning. That summer, after he left school, he began to search for a formal apprenticeship in a kitchen, and he applied to many establishments. It was the classic 'numbers game' approach – writing to as many as possible and seeing who got back to him.

In *The Big Fat Duck Cookbook*, he estimates that he wrote to '20 or so' various establishments. However, it has been suggested elsewhere that he wrote to as many as 40. Likewise, the number of places that replied varies according to different accounts, but is thought to be no more than three at the most. What is agreed is that he only received one positive reply. It came from Le Manoir aux Quat'Saisons, run by Raymond Blanc.

Blanc was born in Besancon in eastern France, not far from Burgundy. His mother Maman Blanc was a fine cook and lovingly served up superb, tasty and healthy meals to her family. When Blanc moved to England, his own career truly took off. He began work at the Rose Revived restaurant as a junior. Then, one day, the head chef was ill and Blanc seized his chance, taking over for the day. He quickly impressed. By 1977, Blanc and his wife had opened their first establishment together – Les Quat'Saisons in Oxford. It had been a huge financial risk to open the restaurant, but it quickly paid off. It won the Egon Ronay Restaurant of the Year and Michelin stars among other awards and distinctions. Four years after opening their first restaurant, they opened a bakery, also in Oxford, called Maison Blanc. Again, it quickly became a hugely successful establishment.

In 1984, he opened Le Manoir aux Quat'Saisons in Oxfordshire, which quickly was awarded two Michelin stars. 'His house is as beautiful as a tale of Lewis Carroll,' commented food critic Gilles Pudlowski. It was this establishment that gave Heston the one positive reply from all the applications he sent out to restaurants. Such a poor response rate might have seemed disappointing in one sense, but, lacking any concrete experience or qualifications, Heston was never going to have fared much better. Indeed, the fact that such a prestigious restaurant, run by a rising star chef, was the one that said yes should have been encouraging rather than disappointing.

Over the years, Blanc has helped to nurture and launch the talent of a host of chefs who are now famous, respected names in their own right, including Marco Pierre White, Martin Burge, Michael Caines and Bruno Loubet. He has also guided new faces into food trade success on his BBC television show *The Restaurant*, in which contestants compete in pairs, whether couples, siblings, parent and child or sometimes friends. How much of a role would he have in helping the fledgling talent of Heston?

A short one, as it turned out.

On his first day at Le Manoir, Heston was led into the kitchen and introduced to a huge mound of green beans. He would have to chop the top and bottom off them all. He would later be given another pile of vegetables to chop, trim or peel. Then he would be asked to gut fish or remove the feathers from foul. He had expected to be given some unglamorous tasks but was disappointed all the same. He was hoping to receive more of a rounded apprenticeship, perhaps being involved in the preparation of some dishes from start to finish. He hoped for more responsibility, too. Nowadays, Heston accepts that his expectations back then were unreasonable. He would not give a rookie free rein in his own establishments' kitchens and knows that it was silly of him to expect it at Le Manoir. His impatience quickly contributed to a confrontation with another of the kitchen staff, which saw Heston break with protocol and come to the brink of violence. However, it also led to a great alliance for him.

'Some bloke was having a go at me one day and, not knowing the etiquette, I threatened to smack him one,' Blumenthal recalled in the *Guardian*. 'I heard this voice shout out, "Don't stay over there. Come over here by me."' That voice came from the mouth of Marco Pierre White, a useful ally and a chef who remains a compadre to this day. The pair had different personalities but also have plenty in common. He reappears quite regularly in Heston's story.

However, it soon became clear to Heston that an apprenticeship at Le Manoir was not going to be suitable for him. His ambition and lack of patience meant he was not suited to the slow, gradual and steady education offered by a formal apprenticeship. Displaying the sort of energy and single-mindedness that have dominated his remarkable rise to the top of his profession, he decided to call it a day at Le Manoir. He had been given a week's probation as a precursor to his apprenticeship proper, and, although he knew he could learn much if he stayed on, he decided not to continue when his probation was up. Here was the legacy of those two solitary years, teaching himself the tricks of the trade in his parents' kitchen and poring over the cookbooks in his bedroom. He had become a maverick with ambition, and wanted to fulfil his dreams *his* way – and fast. This was not going to be possible at Le Manoir so, despite being offered a full apprenticeship, he turned it down and went it alone once again. This had not been a decision he took lightly. He searched his soul before coming to the conclusion, asking himself whether it might actually be hard work and commitment that he was fleeing, but ultimately decided to follow his instincts and went off to tread his own path.

He wonders now whether an apprenticeship at a less prestigious kitchen might have seen him hang around longer. 'Going to the Manoir with Raymond Blanc spurred me on, but it spurred me on to go in a different direction,' he told the *Guardian*. 'Maybe if I'd gone to a smaller kitchen and I was a bigger cog in a smaller wheel, I wouldn't have felt the need to go down my own path and maybe I wouldn't have ended up this way.'

Possibly. Given his energy, ambition and maverick nature, it seems unlikely that Heston could have been straitjacketed into going down the conventional route for long. Either way, Le Manoir's loss was the world's gain ultimately. The manner of Heston's leaving was unusual, but set him on the path that led to glory and riches. All he has ever wanted to do, all he ever wants to do, is to wake up in the morning wanting to go to work. It is an aim that has served him well.

A step taken by Heston's parents had simultaneously made a contribution to the development of the masterchef. The Blumenthals had purchased an apartment south of Montpellier in a town called La Motte du Couchant and, the following year, Heston and his parents travelled there and he turned the trip into a culinary exploration. It became an annual tradition for Heston to stay there and live out the dreams he had developed when reading those cookbooks back in his London bedroom. The Blumenthals would drive to the port in England, hop on the ferry to France and drive to their holiday home. There, his adventure would await him. His passion was large, the extent of his energy and curiosity colossal. Heston would travel around the country visiting restaurants, wholesalers and other establishments. He would note how things worked and ask questions, and he was forever taking mental notes. When he got home to England, he would have new ideas, new experiments and a renewed motivation.

And he found new books, too. For it was now that Heston increased his collection of culinary tomes. As he studiously absorbed their words, he found one that spoke his language. As we have seen, Harold McGee's *On Food And Cooking: The Science And Lore Of The Kitchen* transformed Heston's career. McGee is seen as the father of modern science and his disciples are widespread. When *On Food…* was first published in 1986, it was warmly received by the critics. 'Read this wondrous tome,' the *Evening Standard* urged its readers. The *Mail on Sunday* was equally enthusiastic: 'The business – more than you want to know about anything edible.'

Writing in *The Times Literary Supplement*, Paul Levy was similarly impressed. 'There has been no book like this since Alan Davidson's *Oxford Companion to Food*,' he wrote, 'and there a few books so comprehensive, perspicuous or gracefully written on any subject. It is no exaggeration to call it a masterpiece.' Christopher Hirst of the *Independent* chipped in with his own praise: 'For the price of a meal, you'll get a lifetime's nutrition,' he wrote.

Those reviews guaranteed McGee a loyal and large army of readers, Heston among them. In fact, he later picked *On Food…* as his book of shipwrecked choice when he was on the BBC Radio 4 show *Desert Island Discs*.

He first bought *On Food…* soon after its publication and lapped up what he found in its pages. As we have seen, the 'question everything' principle that Heston is now so famous for solidified in his mind as he read the book. Now, he feels that this principle should have been obvious without McGee's intervention. Yet it was only after the American author had pointed it out that it changed the world of cooking – not least in Heston's kitchen. A metaphorical banner was unveiled across it. It was not that he threw the rule book out of the window, more that he no longer lived by it without question. He had always been a curious, experimental chef but now he felt emboldened to test out more. 'I would try doing a dish 30 different ways,' he told *The Times*. 'With ice cream, I would analyse why you need eggs, why it needs to be whipped, what is the optimum consistency. Inquisitiveness was a key feature.'

Another key moment in his self-teaching came when he studied Nicholas Kurti's lecture, *The Physicist in the Kitchen*. A Hungarian-born physicist who lived in Oxford, Kurti had enjoyed a colourful life. He had to flee antisemitism on a number of occasions and then worked on the Manhattan Project to build and test the first atomic bomb. In his spare time, Kurti loved to cook and his interest in all things culinary eventually led to his marrying his work passion (physics) and his hobby (food) into the aforementioned lecture to the Royal Society in 1969 which stunned audiences. He used a microwave oven – still a new phenomena at this time – to make interesting dishes in interesting ways. He made meringue in a vacuum chamber, cooked sausages by connecting them to a car battery and produced a reverse-baked Alaska – hot inside, cold outside – cooked in the microwave oven. He also suggested other revolutionary techniques, including syringes to inject rum into mince pies and the use of the proteolytic enzymes in fresh pineapple juice to tenderise meats. The audience was aghast.

Kurti was an eminently quotable man. During the famous lecture, he said, 'The invention of a new dish is of greater importance to the happiness of mankind than the discovery of a new star.' Another much-quoted statement made by Kurti during the lecture, and one which struck a chord with Heston, was: 'It is a sad reflection on our civilisation that, while we measure the temperature in the atmosphere of Venus, we do not know what goes on inside our soufflés.'

This was music to Heston's ears, and he was transfixed by the sort of eccentric recipes and methods that Kurti espoused. Here, once more, was culinary innovation and Heston was devouring every last morsel. To this day, he refers back to the seminal lecture in interviews and other conversations.

As his teens gave way to his twenties, Blumenthal met the woman who was to become his wife, a nurse called Zanna. His future career would only have been hinted at to her from the time they first met. 'When I was 18, 19, 20 and first met my wife, I'd spend as much money as others spent on clothes on a meal,' he said.

All the same, as he has stated many times since, he was not a chef when they first met and therefore the sacrifices that they would subsequently have to make came as news to her. She was supportive to him throughout, though, as we shall see. At home, he occasionally lets her cook but admits that he is terrified by how frantically she chops vegetables. '"That really scares me,' I tell her. "You're going to take the end of your fingers off. Pull your fingers in." My wife will probably say I do interfere but I think I'm pretty good.'

Another thing that became obvious to her in time was that Blumenthal had issues with anger. One key incident stands out in both their memories. They were living with Blumenthal's parents, and a man knocked on the door and began to threaten his father over a dispute concerning property. This would be enormously distressing for anybody, although not everyone would respond in the way that Blumenthal did.

'This guy is shouting through the door saying, "I'm going to break your kneecaps," and my son started crying and I was, "I'm not having this,"' he recalled in an interview with *The Times*. 'So I walked out the room and unlocked the cupboard.' He then pulled a gun out of the cupboard, 'an old Beretta with half-a-dozen cartridges. I just walked back to the door and pulled the trigger. I completely lost it. That was scary – it wasn't an adrenalin rush. Everything slowed down. My wife pulled me back, the gun went up.'

The drama was not over. He ran to his car and continued to chase the men. He had surrendered the gun to his wife by this point but was still armed – this time with a meat cleaver. Astonishingly, the story concluded peacefully. Blumenthal found the men in the car park of the local pub and took them back to his parents' home to resolve the issue over a cup of tea. 'We had a chat,' he said. 'It got sorted. No harm done, but it was the biggest wake-up call I could have had.'

However, Blumenthal's eruption – and its potentially

tragic results – had shaken Zanna. 'It was just getting worse and worse and worse,' he admits now. 'It's a long story but she probably stopped me being jailed twice – actually pulled me back … What was really worrying about the shotgun thing was how calm I felt throughout it all. I felt fantastic. It felt fantastic. Powerful. I thought I could rule the world. That's what scared me most, not that I had the capacity to do that, but that I actually enjoyed doing it. It wasn't a one-off, either. There were other incidents where my wife had to pull me back. I remember her saying, "I saw your eyes change." When I got like that, something altered in me. It was almost as if I put myself in a meditative state, I was so relaxed. I knew that, if I didn't get help, I was going to get myself into serious trouble.'

He continues, 'It was awful but it's easier to talk about now because I've absolutely dealt with it. But it went on for five or six years. What was dangerous was the aggression was going down and the more cold, calculated feeling was getting stronger. It was an uncontrollable feeling and when it starts to feel… good… when that feeling starts to feel really good, it's not good news. What's bizarre is there's a difference between being aggressive and starting to feel good about anger and violence. Zanna read about cranial osteopathy and it just gave me the impetus, although it might have been psychosomatic, to do something about it.'

According to the Sutherland Society, which promotes cranial osteopathy, the technique is 'a refined and subtle type of osteopathic treatment that encourages the release of stresses and tensions throughout the body, including the head. It is a gentle yet extremely effective approach and may be used in a wide range of conditions for people of all ages, from birth to old age.'

Blumenthal had gone to anger therapy after the aforementioned increase in his rage began to also show itself at work. 'There's a point when the service is controlling you, you're not controlling the service. I had a really bad temper. Staff stayed for just a few months.'

But the turning point came after several instances of road rage. 'I remember coming into Bray one day, chasing a car in front of me,' he said. 'The driver wouldn't stop, so I actually had the door of my car open, and was driving and hooting and screaming at him to stop.' He concedes, 'It was slightly psychotic behaviour, so I had to do something about it. It's not as if I don't have a temper. I have a temper that's there, but I've dealt with it. I am so calm now. I don't think I've raised my voice in the kitchen for seven years. When I look back, I think, God, did I really behave like that? At work, there's no excuse for humiliating somebody physically, mentally. If someone has messed up and you bawl them out in public, that can't do them any good.'

It was only later on that he truly grasped what sort of person he had been prior to the treatment and the improvement in his mood. He recalled a day when he, his wife and kids heard a neighbour screaming at his own female partner 'really aggressively'. Blumenthal's wife said to the kids: 'Oh my God, imagine being married to that!' and Jack turned round and said, 'You were.'

Blumenthal: 'Zanna came into the kitchen and said,

"You'll never guess what Jack's just said." And that was just out of the blue.'

In contrast to many of his fellow cooks, Blumenthal is now a calm man, not least when at work. There is no screaming and shouting for him. 'Other chefs have quite a peaceful life away from work and encounter bedlam in the kitchen. For me, it's the other way round. When I'm in the kitchen, it's peace and quiet.'

Of the treatment he underwent, he agrees that it is similar in a sense to how babies are treated. 'That's exactly why my wife thought of it,' he said, laughing. 'Babies cry a lot and it works by relaxing them. It relaxed me and it was a gradual process of controlling the anger. I had a bad temper on me. Now I haven't raised my voice in eight years. Maybe it should have been a psychiatrist, but, at the time, that was enough to help me get a nugget of control on it. From there it was just a case of thinking it all through. Every time I wanted to lose the plot, I had to think, I can control this. The upshot is, I don't remember the last time I lost my temper in the kitchen.'

That said, in the early days of The Fat Duck, the enormity of the challenge ahead of him, and the financial risks he had taken to make it, would put him right on the edge at times. 'It was a situation where I had bitten off more than I could chew and I wasn't in control,' he remembered.

An interviewer once asked him whether he'd ever been so angry that he wanted to kill anyone. 'Ughhh… yessss,' he replied, but was keen to emphasise that it was *not* an urge he had ever acted on. 'No, no, no,' he added.

But The Fat Duck was still in Heston's future. Before he got to Bray, he took a string of far less glamorous jobs in order to make ends meet. One of these was as a 'repo man', he says, which means a debt collector. 'I was all right at it, actually; it was only companies. I had an interesting altercation in Dudley. It was an Indian who denied he owed the money. He then made a call and half-a-dozen of his mates turned up. I gave up with the meagre wage I was on.' He was also an accountant for some time, but he eventually decided it was time to give cooking a go professionally.

To this end, he took a brief restaurant-management course at Leiths School of Food and Wine in Wendell Road, in London. He also did a three-week stint at Canteen, run by Marco Pierre White. Celebrity chef White had opened the premises in 1992, along with actor Michael Caine and London restaurant operator Claudio Pulze. Set in Chelsea Harbour in West London, it has since won Michelin stars. It had 250 covers and was such a busy establishment that, when the printer which was used for orders stopped spitting out paper for longer than a few moments, everybody assumed it had broken rather than there weren't any customers.

This was a perfect learning ground for Blumenthal who was immediately shown just how much pressure there can be on a restaurant kitchen. He had to hit the ground running and he was taken aback by how busy it was on his first day. Then, on his second day, he was working on some cod crust dough when he lost control of what he was doing. The result was that many kilos of the dough were fired around the kitchen, much to the embarrassment of the new boy. All the same, he was learning fast, absorbing knowledge just as his dishes absorbed tastes. Within a couple more days he felt at ease in the Canteen kitchen, and could identify what the latest order was just by listening to the sound of the printer hammering out a different rhythm for each dish, not unlike Morse Code.

He was ready to go it alone and, thanks to a recent purchase, he had just the venue for his first professional solitary venture...

CHAPTER THREE

A FAT CHANCE

In his celebrated humorous novel *Three Men in a Boat*, Jerome K Jerome described Maidenhead as 'too snobby to be pleasant'. However, a short drive southwest from that town is the village of Bray. A regular nominee and winner in the *Britain in Bloom* awards, it is an idyll of lanes, luscious greens, a cricket pitch and war memorial. Here houses do not have numbers but names: Old Corner Cottage, The Old Dutch and Vicarage Cottage. It has a country air about it: signs for pedestrian paths do not say 'No Bikes' but 'No Horses'. (The gate of the red-brick almshouses of Jesus Hospital bears a more stringent entry policy: 'No Vagrants, Hawkers or Dogs'.)

Nowadays, the tranquil village, watched over by a 13th-century parish church, is scarcely disturbed by the fishmongers delivering fresh produce to the two restaurants with three Michelin stars and a pub. Indeed, the morning is not complete without men in chef's uniforms walking down the High Street ready to go to work. The village noticeboard proudly boasts of the presence of the famous Heston Blumenthal. His pastry chef James 'Jocky' Petrie waits for a procession of cars to pass (this being Bray, many have personalised number plates) before striding regally across the road and entering the property which Blumenthal bought in 1995 and turned into one of the world's most famous restaurants.

The Bell in Bray, a 450-year-old pub, was not the first venue viewed by Blumenthal as he sought his first culinary premises. It is an indication of how inappropriate and expensive the other venues must have been that Blumenthal chose to buy The Bell despite knowing of its plentiful flaws. It was not as big as Blumenthal would have liked, it had only one door and it lacked any sort of pleasing view. And these were not the only 'calamitous drawbacks' he noted. It was dirty and the painfully small kitchen was lacking equipment. All the same, after previous attempts to secure a premises had ended in disappointment, he signed on the dotted line and was handed the keys to his first eaterie.

So what was the history of The Bell? Originally known as The Bell Ringers, the venue on Bray High Street has had many owners over the centuries. Among those to have previously had their name above its solitary door were Thomas Christopher, John Martin, Elizabeth Christopher, Richard Tonson and John Hall. No less a personage than the Bishop of Oxford was involved in the property during the 1700s.

At the end of the 19th century, it was leased to a man

called John Fuller for just £40 a year. When Blumenthal purchased it in 1995, there was of course a considerably higher financial outlay. Yet, despite its imperfections, he was pleased with his purchase of The Bell. It had a wooden floor, brick walls and oak beams. These, he felt, gave it a bistro feel and so the French cuisine he was planning to serve would be in an appropriate setting.

A reviewer would later write of the surroundings, 'The Fat Duck occupies the ground floor of a large, low-ceilinged house. With its ancient beams, wooden floors, gothic metal chairs, recessed down-lighters and ochre walls, the decor is, like the food, half-modern, half-rustic.'

The Bell was round the corner from Michel Roux's Waterside Inn restaurant, and Heston hoped that some of the customers who went to eat fine food there might be attracted to his own establishment for some more of the same.

Not that he immediately planned to change the menu. Indeed, once he had rolled up his sleeves and knocked the venue into order, he posted a menu that included the same options that the previous owners had offered. He did not want to immediately turn the old place into one that reflected his vision. Instead, he planned to initially continue doing what the locals were used to. He was told by one of them that the nickname for The Bell was The Magnet because it attracted undesirables who were not allowed into the other public houses in the area. Blumenthal didn't have to wait long to discover that his new business's reputation was well-earned.

Just four days after the restaurant opened under its new

management, a fight broke out in the garden of the pub, and as Blumenthal looked on in shock he noticed a knife being drawn. The brawl threatened to spill over into something far more serious. The police were called and swiftly broke things up. All the same, the fight had shaken Blumenthal to the core. He had planned to wait at least a month until closing for refurbishment but decided to bring that process forward in the wake of the violence he had witnessed.

In doing so, he decided to change the official name of the venue. Various French titles were suggested but Blumenthal was determined that his venue would have an English moniker. He also wanted a name that reflected the pub's longstanding history. The Innkeeper and The Beer Garden were among the suggestions, the latter coming from his friend Marco Pierre White. Blumenthal's own father chipped in with The Far Quenelle. A witty suggestion but one that Blumenthal felt proved that the discussions were losing focus. Some more parameters were set: for instance, he wanted the name to reflect the venue's riverside location. Eventually, they settled on The Fat Duck. Blumenthal says that White claims credit for the name and, although he cannot recall for definite who came up with it, he is happy to accredit it to his friend. He later quipped that, just like a duck which appears serene on the surface but is paddling like mad below water, his early customers would be presented with a calm scene in the dining room which belied the chaos of the kitchen.

Meanwhile, the refit continued apace. Heston did what he could to improve the small kitchen, including putting in a new sink, fridge and oven. However, the cramped surroundings made it hard to do much in the way of improvements. However, more could be done in the dining room, where Blumenthal's attention to detail and eccentric approach to his work began to show itself. When the wooden floors were sandblasted, Blumenthal told the workers to leave it with an imperfect finish, although they took some persuading, as they felt he was setting out to undermine them. But he had a vision.

A French-style bar was installed in the middle of the dining room. It had been designed by his cousin and had a duck theme to it thanks to overlapping pieces of copper which resembled feathers. Blumenthal was happy as his vision for the refit proceeded and took shape. He recalls how symbolic it seemed when he removed the last of the original bar and dumped it outside in a skip. He also recalls an interesting encounter at that moment. An elderly, posh local woman was walking past and, on a natural high of enthusiasm as his dreams took shape, he approached her because here, he felt, was the embodiment of the sort of customer he wanted to attract.

Brimming with enthusiasm, he told her all about the new restaurant he was putting together for the locals. His monologue was speedily delivered, excitable and passionate – who could fail to be won over by such zeal? When he finally paused for breath, the lady told him, 'There have been three owners in the past five years. We have closed them down and we will close you down too.' And off she went, waving her walking stick in the air as she talked to herself.

Welcome to Bray, and welcome to the reality of opening a new business.

There was another wake-up call just days later when Blumenthal found a letter from Bray parish council sitting on his doormat in the morning. On opening the envelope, he discovered that the parish council wanted to oppose the choice of The Fat Duck as the name for the venue as it was 'considered to be quite inappropriate in a village like Bray'. A knife-fight, a promise that locals would close him down and a complaint about the name he had chosen: it was a less than welcoming start for The Fat Duck.

Once he reopened the doors, he hoped, the local opposition would dissolve. He would have enough to be dealing with in the restaurant as it was. There were some chaotic moments in the early days – the early years, in fact, which he himself described as 'bedlam and chaos' in *The Big Fat Duck Cookbook*. In the cramped kitchen there was plenty of excitement, from the second evening which he spent with a bag of peas held to his head and a friend following his precise instructions on the preparation of dishes. The awkward state of affairs had come about after he lit a match to ignite the oven and an explosion sent him flying across the room with a burned face and his hair on fire. Then there was the time that the fryer caught light. Blumenthal surprised his wife Zanna when he carried on cooking while a colleague put the flames out. He was ever the focused professional, though he had great personal support from Zanna.

She was a key factor in Blumenthal's great ascent in the

industry and as the Fat Duck first showed its plumage. 'She is the single biggest reason for my success,' he has said, always keen to acknowledge her role. 'We were saving, saving, saving, then going to France and blowing the money eating. She was a nurse and had never experienced fine dining but she loved it, too. Our mates thought it absurd. We even flogged the car – an awful, lilac-blue Proton – so we could go to France. I didn't have a plan, but, as long as I was cooking, she was happy. We moved house a lot during the early days, but I was always too busy at work even to be there for the flit, never mind help pack up. Once, I got confused and actually went home to the wrong house. That's how divorced from the nitty-gritty I was.'

He had to be alert to anything that might happen in the Duck – no more so than when a venture involving a cake went disastrously wrong at the last moment, after weeks of preparation. A lady had booked The Fat Duck for her husband's 40th birthday and asked Blumenthal to prepare a birthday cake for the occasion. Week after week, she would phone with more instructions as to what ingredients the cake should, and should not, contain. It stretched the already madly busy Blumenthal to the limit. Miraculously, he managed to produce a cake that he felt matched her exacting specifications. On the day that the lady and her husband arrived, he opened the fridge that the cake was resting on and the cake slid off the top and landed on the floor. With not a moment to lose, he phoned Michel Roux who had, by amazing and happy coincidence, a cake that fitted the complicated bill.

His staff in those days was made up of a varied bunch of characters. One employee was a huge man who had done time in an army prison and was covered in tattoos. But it didn't matter what they looked like – everyone had to commit to the long and hard hours that The Fat Duck demanded. A joke quickly started up. If a staff member noticed anything going wrong, he or she would quip, 'I'm just going to the bank.' This was in response to the abrupt departure of a staff member who one day told colleagues he was going to the bank and was never seen again. And he wasn't the only one who left in less than ideal circumstances. A key member of the team departed after an upset in his personal life meant that he ceased to pay attention to his duties. It culminated in him complaining about the 'fucking customers' – regularly and audibly.

Of course, just as he had to fire on occasion, he regularly had to hire. His interviewing technique was unconventional. He would sometimes be working in the kitchen as he conducted the interviews and was known on some occasions to do more talking than his interviewees. One such hopeful later told Blumenthal, 'You interviewed me for an hour as you worked, talking nonstop about protein and denaturing and electron exchange and radiation. I didn't understand a word and figured… this has got to be good.'

As word got round the industry what was happening at The Fat Duck, Blumenthal received unsolicited job enquiries from chefs willing to work there.

One of his most impressive early chefs was a man called Garrey Dawson, who had begun his career at Pennyhill Park

Hotel in Surrey, where he worked between 1988 and 1992. He then spent four years at Cliveden Hotel as commis chef in the sauce and vegetable section of the star-rated Waldo's restaurant. Dawson arrived at The Fat Duck, having turned down an offer from Le Manoir in favour of the opportunity to work with Blumenthal. It was proof of the reputation that was already building up in the chef fraternity. Dawson proved to be an extraordinarily hard worker and an entertaining one, too. As he and his team worked long and hard in the kitchen, he kept their spirits buoyed. 'Less chit-chat, more chop-chop,' was one of the catchphrases he used when he felt his team needed to step it up a gear. He could also make people laugh when they needed it, not least by regularly asking random questions of his team. One day he asked them how many of them had worn their wife's underwear, for instance. He was an optimistic, enthusiastic head chef, and, when it came to the nuts and bolts of the job itself, he was fantastic at giving the level of attention to detail that Blumenthal admired. Like Blumenthal, Dawson has since found fame on BBC's *Ready, Steady, Cook*.

Dawson was succeeded at The Fat Duck by a man called Ashley Palmer-Watts, who had joined the team soon after he had eaten at the restaurant to celebrate his 21st birthday. 'It is difficult to explain, but I felt drawn to the place,' he said. 'It was very different then from how it is now – the meal we had was quite rustic and hearty and there was no tasting menu – but it was distinct from anywhere else.'

He has always enjoyed working with Blumenthal. 'Working with Heston is truly inspirational. As well as his constant drive for perfecting food and getting the best out of ingredients without over-complicating dishes, he is also a fun and exciting person to be with. He constantly inspires enjoyment among the staff in what we do and in the experience of eating here among the customers.'

Blumenthal repaid the compliment. 'He will not compromise perfection and is fastidious in his attention to detail,' he said of Palmer-Watts. 'His enthusiasm and assistance with my menu research and development work is fundamental. It is imperative that continuity is maintained in a restaurant like The Fat Duck and, as my head chef, I have always been able to rely on Ashley one hundred per cent. He is an invaluable member of the team.'

Just as Dawson had a catchphrase from early on, so did his successor. Palmer-Watts would regularly exhort his team to 'push on'. Soon other staff members came up with their own memorable sayings. One would encourage colleagues with a shout of 'hit it' and, as for Blumenthal himself, his became 'I reckon' – two words he used with noticeable regularity. They came up with their own words for dishes, as the team spirit increased. Bonds were formed through their catchphrases and private language. Blumenthal, ever the observant one, noticed individual quirks and tics that his staff had. He could predict after how many chops on a chopping board each cook would tap the knife to clean it. He could tell you which staff members found it impossible to pass a pan without giving it a quick agitation. He could even tell you which one he once saw shake an empty pan.

This, then, was the atmosphere in the cramped kitchen of

The Fat Duck in the early years of the restaurant's existence. But what was on the menu? An early menu shows that starters included herb and leaf salad, haricot blanc soup, chicken liver and foie gras parfait with fig compote. Among the main courses were salmon, puy lentils, pea and horseradish sauce, steak and chips with sauce a la moelle and roast rump of lamb, ratatouille and gratin of potatoes with epoisses. The desserts included poached pear with red wine sorbet, chocolate tart and jasmine tea and orange flower water creme brulee. However, the most popular dish in these days was the *petit sale* of duck with pommes puree, with customers enjoying the chance to sit in a restaurant called The Fat Duck, next to a river populated by ducks and eat a duck. It was a dish that took nearly 40 hours to produce and customers appreciated the effort. As did reviewers, with the *Independent*'s Emily Green describing the dish as 'a main course I would travel for'.

That said, she was not without criticism of some of its features. 'The only problem with the duck was the mash that accompanied it: this pommes puree was made the hard and long way, but managed to come out tasting a bit glutinous, as if it had been passed in a blender,' she wrote, though she was quick to return to praise. 'Far better, spuds-wise, were the chips with steak and chips. These were terrific: chunky, blazing hot, perfectly seasoned, really crisp outside, melting within. Best chips ever, maybe. The steak was good too.'

It was not just the food that impressed her, she was also full of praise for the interior, describing it as 'a remarkably pleasant place. It seems fitting that it is in Bray, the heart of Roux country, a near neighbour of one of Britain's oldest three-stars, the Waterside Inn. And it is a relief that The Fat Duck is not an overly swanky restaurant, rather a pretty conversion of an old pub. A somewhat ancient, beamed room has been painted a fresh white and furnished with a simple and pleasing assembly of tables and chairs. A bar made from hammered copper lends the place lustre, and there are ladylike decorative touches, such as the strategic placement here and there of large terracotta urns of the sort one sees in Liberty's gardening section, or in books about ancient Greece. These are pretty vessels, if not my sort of junk. The showpiece that caught my eye was a first-class cheese board, set on a fine old table.'

In conclusion, wrote Green, 'This might seem a high price to pay a beginner. Certainly any recommendation of The Fat Duck should be accompanied by the warning: the Heston Blumenthal school of catering is as dicey as it is eccentric ... the £45 I paid him produced that rare and pleasurable thing, a remarkably good meal.'

The following year, Ben Rogers also reviewed The Fat Duck for the same newspaper. He feared that he had been identified as a journalist when a simple query to a waiter drew Blumenthal himself from the kitchen. 'I first began to suspect the staff at The Fat Duck knew my true identity when my request to find out what gave the foie gras its slightly nutty flavour drew the chef and proprietor, Heston Blumenthal, from his kitchen. (It was due, he explained, to a particularly almondy sherry that he uses, although I was not sure, while we are on the subject, that the nuttiness added to the dish.) I still don't know quite what gave me away, but I put it down to my photographer, who broke all the rules by venturing into the field before me.' Whether or not he had been identified as a reviewer, Rogers noted, all customers were equally treated well. 'We, of course, were well looked after, but it was clear other customers were being treated just as handsomely by the charming and enthusiastic staff,' he said. 'Blumenthal needs, though, to work on his menu, which is awkwardly written, badly punctuated, and at points quite impenetrable. (What is 'ballontine of confit duck's neck, prunes and Armagnac, potatoes and gizzards confit'?)'

They were not the only food critics to write up The Fat Duck in its early days. Scribes from the *Guardian* and the *Evening Standard* attended too, both going on to print positive reviews. The latter journal sent Fay Maschler, who published her review in November 2006. Blumenthal had been nervous to read it, since he felt that Maschler was perhaps the critic whose viewpoint he most respected and because he feared that the glaze on the *petit sale* had been wrong on the day she visited. He need not have been concerned: 'Energy and invention are sustained in the dessert course with ideas such as salted-butter caramel with cacao sorbet, and with experimentation such as the use of jasmine tea and orange flower water to flavour a creme brulee,' she wrote. 'The pub has been stylishly, quirkily rendered a restaurant and the sophisticated management and service give it a pleasingly foreign feel. There is no view of the river, but in pretty weather a courtyard at the back is brought into play.'

She also praised Blumenthal personally. 'Heston Blumenthal, chef/patron of The Fat Duck has chutzpah, it must be said, in taking on the culinary vicar of Bray, Michel Roux at The Waterside Inn,' she penned. 'All the more so since – except for a short stint in the kitchen of Marco Pierre White – Blumenthal is self-taught. Inspiration, he says, comes from reading and eating when travelling in France and he cites Alain Chapel and Michel Bras as particular mentors. The dishes on the relatively short menu, although traceable to certain influences (including Roux), are singular. Like a scientist balancing an equation or a novelist polishing a sentence, Blumenthal seems to have worked and reworked his ideas until something approaching perfection is achieved.'

With both his restaurant and he himself being so positively received, he could afford to smile. Those worries about the glaze on the *petit sale* could be forgotten.

Blumenthal was garnering lots of positive press and his confidence was growing accordingly. The Fat Duck was going swimmingly, one could say. The *Guardian*'s Matthew Fort said that the starters of foie gras parfait and the marinade of mackerel 'fulfilled their possibilities to perfection, and so it went with the main courses'. He is now a major advocate of the restaurant and has returned many times. He has written further reviews and became very familiar to Blumenthal, with the pair often talking for hours about cooking.

As the profile of the restaurant increased in the late 1990s, so did the number of customers. The food was always improving and, in 1998, three years after he first bought the venue, Blumenthal was hopeful that The Fat Duck would be awarded its first Michelin star. In *The Big Fat Duck Cookbook*, he accepts that in retrospect his expectation was naive. After all, the dining room had no tablecloths and diners had to walk through a yard to visit the toilets. All the same, he was constantly upping his game and admits that in that year he 'half' expected to get a star. It was not to be. He wouldn't, though, have to wait much longer for the much-anticipated moment.

In 1999, things began to go from strength to strength at The Fat Duck, and he received his first Michelin star. In *The Big Fat Duck Cookbook*, he says that when he was told of the news it was a 'tremendous feeling' and added that he was 'absolutely thrilled'. He thought back to those summers that he spent driving round France to visit the restaurants that he had read about in his *Michelin Guide*. Now he ran just such a restaurant, albeit in the heart of England.

'There is simply nothing like the emotion that overwhelms you,' he wrote, describing how he felt on the day that he received a crisp new edition of the *Michelin Guide* and saw his own restaurant, The Fat Duck, on its pages. Here he achieved a major goal. Just as many foodstuffs transported him back to his past, so did his Michelin moment. He connected back with the younger man who had pored over the pages of that book in his bedroom, dreaming of merely being able to eat in such restaurants, let alone actually own and run one. The hard work and the sacrifices that not just he but his entire family had made were starting to pay off. One such sacrifice made by his wife he humorously recalled later: 'I woke [Zanna] up at 2am once, with four different creme brulees I'd made. That put her off creme brulee for quite a while.' A less happy one was missing the birth of his second child, Jessie, in 2005. 'Our second child, Jessie, was born the year the restaurant opened. I couldn't be there for her birth.'

As a result of the Michelin star, business boomed even further. A celebrity visitor came in the shape of Irish chatshow legend Terry Wogan. Tracey Macleod – who first met Wogan when she was a researcher on his television show in the mid-1980s – took him to The Fat Duck for lunch one day and wrote up the experience in the *Independent*. The pair had a great meal with only the seating raising any significant criticism. 'I'm glad you asked me here – I've wanted to try it for a while, but I can never get a table,' Wogan told Macleod, as 'he attempted to settle his comfortably-upholstered frame into one of The Fat Duck's rather less comfortably-upholstered iron chairs'. She might have been critical of the chairs, but the overall scene left her impressed. 'Converted from a pub, the restaurant's low ceilings, roughly-finished cream walls and coir flooring give it a homely, countrified atmosphere which belies the sophisticated polish of its food,' she wrote of the interior.

Wogan, she revealed, kicked off with 'a thick tranche of roasted foie gras, served with seasidey accompaniments of marinated raw salmon, a crisp crab biscuit, crystallised seaweed and a pureed oyster sauce'. He was impressed. 'The foie is beautifully cooked, and that's very hard to do when it's such a thick piece,' he told his fellow diner. He was impressed, too, by the supporting ingredients, 'though I tend to think foie gras should be served very simply, just crisped on either side, with probably a sweet or piquant counterbalance'.

'Service was exemplary', she reported, 'informed without being intrusive.' As they said their goodbyes, she asked Wogan if he would be returning to The Fat Duck. 'I would, but not on the basis of the chairs,' he replied. 'Still, that's my one criticism. It's a very pretty place, and he's obviously a good and original chef.'

Blumenthal will no doubt have smiled at those words.

And he had even more to smile at. Wogan's visit – and complaint that he found it hard to book a table – both came in the wake of the post-Michelin upsurge in trade. Blumenthal noticed an increase in weekend trade in particular, while he also found that he could recruit new staff more easily. Customers and cooks were now even keener on the idea of getting involved in The Fat Duck experience as Blumenthal turned from disciple to leader. However, the Michelin star was only the beginning of what he had in mind. Ever curious, ambitious and enthusiastic, Blumenthal was heading onwards and upwards to even greater glories.

In *The Big Fat Duck Cookbook*, Blumenthal describes his first signature dish as crab biscuit, roast foie gras and oyster vinaigrette. It originally involved sliced salmon but the fish was soon replaced by rhubarb. He also experimented with many forms of crab and finally settled on one from Brittany in France. Then came experimentation over which liquid to poach the crab in – they eventually settled for plain old water. With the line-up complete, he was ready to present the dish to the world. He describes the sensation of first serving this, his first-ever signature dish, as being akin to taking a bungee jump: an extraordinary mixture of excitement and fear. It met with approval and captured the imagination of the media, too.

As Nikki Spencer wrote in the *Independent*, 'One of Heston's signature dishes at his famous Berkshire restaurant is fine crab biscuits layered with foie gras, marinated salmon and crystallised seaweed with an oyster vinaigrette. Also popular is a potage of laitue de mer (sea lettuce) with poached oyster.'

He had a good relationship with the *Independent*, and as early as 1997 he was quoted in a feature in the paper about the growing use of seaweed in cooking. 'The thing about seaweed is that you can't really eat a big plate of it on its own but its very distinctive flavour means that it can certainly enhance a dish,' he said.

However, it was through a rival newspaper that he made a new connection. When he finished writing his recipe book *Family Food*, Blumenthal asked his longstanding literary ally Matthew Fort to read the introduction and offer feedback and tips. Fort liked what he found and arranged for Blumenthal to write a column for the *Guardian*. Once more, Blumenthal found himself getting carried away with enthusiasm as he wrote. The brief for the column was that it should run to 1,200 words each week, but it was not unheard of for him to file as many as double that figure. His words were edited to fit the bill and his first column was soon on its way to the printers. So it was that on 10 November 2001 he picked up a copy of the famous broadsheet and opened it to find his first ever newspaper column. It was a proud moment for Blumenthal and his family. And of course his fame was to rocket in the coming years.

Blumenthal was ready to broaden his media profile with a television show. The Discovery Channel commissioned Blumenthal to produce six 30-minute shows for a series called *Kitchen Chemistry*. There he worked with Peter Barham, who explained on the show's website how they met and built up a rapport. 'It soon became apparent that we shared a common philosophy – that the application of science to cooking can only improve our techniques and experiences. Thus we started working together. Heston and I meet every few weeks to talk about the science of food and cooking. Usually the conversations start with some specific issue. Maybe one of Heston's chefs has noticed something odd in the kitchen, maybe I've read about some new and interesting scientific discovery, maybe there has been some problem in the kitchen and Heston wants to ensure that in future the problem is solved. But always, we end up talking about many other issues sparking off new ideas for cooking processes and dishes, etc. Obviously, much of this comes to nothing, but a few ideas lead to real novel developments. Our collaboration has been very fruitful and influential. Heston is widely recognised as one of the UK's top chefs so his interest in applying science in all his cooking has given molecular gastronomy credibility in the catering industry. Perhaps the most important aspects of our collaborations are the development of new cooking methods and the use of scientific equipment in the kitchen which have led to the appearance of completely new dishes on his menu.'

The show was directed by Mark Halliley and the series was an entertaining and educational affair. It garnered Blumenthal his first-ever television write-up from no less than the catty Victor Lewis-Smith, who described Blumenthal's face in close-ups as 'like an ambulance man peering at you through your letterbox after you've had the near-fatal stroke'. Blumenthal, known for his sense of humour, must not have been offended by this less than flattering turn of phrase, for he voluntarily quoted it in *The Big Fat Duck Cookbook*.

Around this time, more and more reviewers and other journalists began to appear at The Fat Duck. One came from as far away as America, a journalist from one of the best-known newspapers in the world. RW Apple Junior wrote up his experiences in the *New York Times*. 'My wife Betsey and I ate our Easter dinner at The Fat Duck this year and, in keeping with the season, Mr Blumenthal suggested that we order some lamb as a main course,' he wrote. 'As it turned out, we were the designated guinea pigs for one of his latest experiments, an innovative way of cooking lamb.' They were delighted with the results. Apple Junior was full of praise for Blumenthal's professional ambition and courage. 'Choosing to start a restaurant in Bray took a lot of nerve,' he wrote.

'The Fat Duck is just a few blocks from the Waterside Inn, the gilded stage on which Michel Roux, a great French classicist, has for many years done his three-star turn. At first, Mr Blumenthal stuck with simple things – rillettes of salmon, steak frites, lemon tart – but what a tart and what frites! Chubby little things, fried to crisp perfection, stacked like Lincoln Logs [toys]. They still arrive with the veal kidney roasted in its own fat.'

He reviewed the history of the restaurant to date and then made predictions for the future, not all of which pleased him. 'Until now, the Duck itself has remained unchanged – two plain rooms, no tablecloths, stainless-steel cutlery, beamed ceilings, wrought-iron tables and chairs, and a long, shiny copper bar. Too plain, some say, for the prices. Dinner can easily run $85, without wine or tip, although there is a far from meagre three-course set lunch for $37.50. Changes in decor are on the way, including, to my great regret, the elimination of the bar to make room for a place for pre- and post-dinner drinks. That was inevitable, I guess; although this year's *Good Food Guide* ranks The Fat Duck among the top dozen country restaurants in England and one of its inspectors reported that the three best meals that he ate in 1999 were all at the Duck, *Michelin* still gives it only one lonely star. For larger constellations, the red M demands a certain degree of luxury.'

The Fat Duck would indeed go on to receive more Michelin stars, but it would do so without having to make as many compromises as Apple Junior predicted.

The scribe was correct, though, that many changes were

afoot at the restaurant. It wasn't long into the new century that Blumenthal closed the venue for four weeks and called in a raft of experts and workers, including fibre-optic specialists, to create a new and improved restaurant. He introduced carpet to the dining-room floors, an inside toilet and – for the first time – the tables were given tablecloths. Heston also arranged a second refit for the kitchen. There was nothing he could do to make the room itself any larger, but he could make it a far more agreeable and functional atmosphere by introducing new hardware and new fridges and with imaginative ways of creating more space. Among the other improvements were new gas pipes. He had previously had such slim pipes that rudimentary kitchen tasks such as boiling a pan of water were proving agonisingly time-consuming affairs. The fresh pipes were thicker and far more powerful, befitting a professional kitchen.

The new-look Fat Duck reopened and proved a more agreeable place for both customers and staff, although the first customers arrived while the carpet was still being fitted upstairs after a last-minute panic. A previous floor covering shipped in from the Far East had proved inappropriate. Blumenthal had been careful to make sure that the new comfortable features did not compromise the personality of the restaurant, and overall he was pleased with his efforts.

However, during the four weeks that the Fat Duck was closed, perhaps the biggest development that Blumenthal worked on was what the restaurant is now most famous for – its tasting menu. He attentively perused scientific hardware catalogues to this end, poring over the products inside, many of which had not been designed with any sort of culinary use in mind. To Blumenthal, ever the open-minded experimenter, *anything* could potentially be turned into a kitchen tool. During the break, he was an inspired, almost possessed figure at home, to be seen with his nose in a catalogue or surrounded by a crazy connection of test tubes in his kitchen at home. His obsessive, eccentric behaviour was noted by Zanna, who would encourage him to switch off at night by reading something unconnected to his work.

One of the experiments he was working on involved cooking salmon in a water bath called a bain-marie. A French invention, it was used to heat items at a consistent temperature. After more feverish experimentation and investigation, he introduced vacuum packaging to the process and found he could achieve even more acute control over the process. A key part of Fat Duck process and folklore had been born. As ever, for the adventurous Blumenthal, this was just the beginning of the matter.

One of the first dishes to grace the tasting menu line-up was nitro-poached green tea and lime sour, which Blumenthal had worked on during the closure of the restaurant in August and September 2000. As would so often be the case in his career, Blumenthal initially came across the idea for this dish as a result of an everyday thought. A quandary, in fact. As a diner, he enjoyed being able to arrive at the table with a fresh mouth and palate, so he could truly appreciate what he was about to eat. However, simply brushing his teeth prior to sitting down was not an option, as he found that the taste of toothpaste stayed in his mouth and therefore compromised his enjoyment of the meal. If only, he thought as he sweated along in his experimentation, he could kick off his nascent tasting menu with a dish that freshened up the taste buds without lingering and interfering with the meal ahead.

As a starting point, he telephoned scientist Tony Blake, a professor who is a global authority on flavour and taste, and asked his advice. Blake told Blumenthal that green tea was an effective palate cleanser. The research that had made this discovery was suitably eccentric: Japanese students had eaten garlic, chewed a green-tea-based chewing gum and then breathed into the nose of the scientist from close-up. Armed with this knowledge, Blumenthal set about experimenting on how to get a green-tea blend that was the perfect strength. Another part of his investigation was to introduce an element that would, quite literally, get the customers' juices flowing at the start of the meal. To this end, he added lime juice and malic acid to the mix. However, the next step in the genesis of this dish was to be the most extraordinary.

The use of liquid nitrogen is a cooking method that has become synonymous with Blumenthal. Though he credits predecessors with its introduction into the gastronomic scene, he is at the heart of its use. It is believed that The Fat Duck was, for instance, the first restaurant to employ it. Liquid nitrogen is very cold – minus 196 degrees Celsius – and his initial experiments with the substance gave him a first-hand encounter with just how cold this is. After dipping a banana in liquid nitrogen, he foolishly held it to his mouth and suffered frostbite on his lip, much to the amusement of his colleagues.

However, as word spread around Bray that Blumenthal was experimenting with liquid nitrogen, an atmosphere of a different emotion spread: fear. Just getting the all-clear from his environmental health officer to use it had been a task involving much local reassurance. He then received correspondence from a teacher at a nearby catering college warning him that its use carried a danger of explosion. Naturally, Blumenthal had already carefully researched any danger that it might pose, and had even spoken to his hero Harold McGee. In fact, the only damage it caused was to Blumenthal's bank balance. The kit to make it cost over £1,000 a time and, as the staff served the dish at the tables, the liquid nitrogen evaporated at a tremendous rate, meaning The Fat Duck was requiring hundreds of litres of the costly product every month. The ingredients of the dish were further refined, as was the way it was served and the hardware. Yet by the time it made its debut, nitro-poached green tea and lime mousse was a multi-sensory experience to delight diners at the outset of the tasting experience.

As for the menu itself, it produced a new challenge for Blumenthal. Some guests would stay with the a la carte, but to cater for those who went for the tasting option the small kitchen had to be ready to face the potential for increasing the amount of dishes it produced fivefold. He admits now that he did not know until the reopening whether the whole scheme would work. The first incarnation was launched in

2000, a modest affair of seven dishes compared to the 20-plus dishes it now contains. At the time, though, it was an exciting innovation. It kicked off with green tea and lime sour and completed with petit fours which included chocolate infused with pipe tobacco. In between, the world began to see more of the inventive eccentricity that Blumenthal is now famed for. The crab risotto included red pepper cassonade, crab ice cream and passion-fruit jelly. There was pineapple and chilli jelly, too. Imaginative, thought-provoking dishes.

Popular dishes, too, it turned out. Customers still had the option to order a more conventional a la carte meal but many were opting for the tasting menu. He had captured – and to an extent shaped – a new spirit of culinary adventure in the UK prompted and then reflected by a surge in the number of cookery shows on television, food sections in newspapers and features in magazines. The public was after original tastes and experiences and didn't Heston know it, as more and more orders for the tasting menu were relayed into the Fat Duck kitchen.

So how did the kitchen perform with the new demands? Well, it managed... but sometimes only just. It was a complicated process for sure and, as Blumenthal crashed out at the end of busy nights, he would sip a beer and wonder what he had got himself into with the tasting menu. He would even ask himself whether he had taken an ambitious step too far.

Still, the popularity of the tasting menu was welcome, whatever organisational challenges it threw up for

Blumenthal. As ever, his faithful ally Matthew Fort was quick to offer his own professional literary praise for the dishes, writing, 'These dishes resolve themselves brilliantly on the palate. Each mouthful calls into action a range of sensations through the interplay between hot and cold, sweet and sour, fruit and savoury, one texture and another... I won't bore you by detailing the almost endless list of felicities of each dish. This is supremely considered cooking of awesome technical accomplishment.' Encouraging words indeed.

However, the admiration came from far and wide as Blumenthal became better known. In the *Independent*, celebrity chef Antony Worrall Thompson cited 'The Fat Duck's Heston Blumenthal as the one to watch in 2001'. Thompson described him as 'probably the best chef in the country. He's already got one Michelin star; he deserves two, if not three. He's as good as [Ferran] Adrià at El Bulli.'

Victoria Moore of the *Guardian* visited Blumenthal at his workplace. Her resultant feature gave a good insight into his restaurant and mood at this time. 'Some people just start laughing when they read our menu,' Blumenthal told her. 'They think it's a joke.' However, as Moore reported, he was not having a joke. Quite the opposite, she wrote: 'This menu is deadly serious. And 34-year-old Blumenthal is not the only one who thinks so ... Close friend Marco Pierre White has called him "an exceptional young man", adding that he expects Blumenthal will soon win a second [Michelin] star. And the current *Good Food Guide* fetes him as chef of the year.' Having sampled some of his dishes, she went on herself to describe Blumenthal as 'the Willy Wonka of modern

British cooking. If his food sounds like the kind of food people politely like to call "challenging", then believe me, it's not, for the simple reason that you don't have to try hard to enjoy it. Blumenthal's are some of the cleanest, yet most intense, flavours you will ever taste. And the combinations of tastes are revelatory, blowing away all preconceptions about what one should eat when.'

She did not only eat his food, but also observed him preparing it. 'In his tiny kitchen at The Fat Duck, I watch entranced as he churns one absurd-sounding ice cream after another (wholegrain mustard; chocolate and thyme; bacon),' she penned. 'Someone else is whizzing a frozen cauliflower puree through a machine that grinds it to a fine crystalline powder ("to make it smoother"). Another is patiently monitoring electronic temperature prods stuck in venison fillets that are being very slowly pan-cooked and turned by hand every couple of minutes. On a shelf I notice a canister of liquid nitrogen that, I am told, is sprayed on foie gras to keep the outer surface cool so that it can cook evenly all the way through. At the helm of all this, in his spattered green trousers, strawberry-blonde hair shorn to frame a genial face, Heston Blumenthal is calm.'

The man at the helm of The Fat Duck kitchen was soon to be further recognised by his peers. At the end of 2002, as reported in *Caterer* magazine, he was honoured with a very special gong. 'Revolutionary chef Heston Blumenthal, of The Fat Duck in Bray, Berkshire, has been named the Chefs' Chef 2002 in the forthcoming *AA Restaurant Guide*,' read the report.

The title he had been awarded was decided in a poll of 1800 chefs in Britain, based on nominations from Marco Pierre White; Simon Wright, editor of the *Restaurant Guide*; other AA guide inspectors and *Caterer and Hotelkeeper* editor Amanda Afiya. Marco Pierre Wright was clear about why Blumenthal deserved the award. 'I think it's not just a great credit to Heston that he was chosen but also to the chefs for choosing him and understanding what he's about,' he said. 'The excitement of his cooking can take your breath away, but it's built on the same foundations as any other great cooking: quality ingredients and accuracy. Anyone thinking about emulating him, who is attracted by the more electric and eye-catching elements of what he does, would do well to bear that in mind.'

It was not just famous chefs such as White who had voted, it was also everyday cooks who slogged away in their kitchens outside the celebrity chef world. One such man was Richard Guest, the head chef at the Castle hotel in Taunton. 'What [Blumenthal] has achieved can only create interest and hunger in young chefs, something for them to aspire to and learn from. With passion like his, people will listen, and perhaps learn completely new ways of preparation, cooking and presentation.'

The man who won the award was modest in receiving it. Blumenthal described the news as 'fantastic'. He added, 'I don't quite understand why I've got it and I don't want to be put on a pedestal, but obviously it's great to be recognised by your peers.' He was not merely modest, but also realistic. Despite his recognition, he accepted that there would always be some who will remain opposed to his style. 'I think I'm always going to get some criticism, but I know that we are infinitely better than we were four months ago, and in a year's time we will be better still,' he said. 'We're just such a young restaurant – we're not even halfway through our lifetime.'

Speaking to the *Telegraph*, he was similarly focused on the long term and confident in his ambitions. 'I think this is the beginning of a whole new approach to cooking,' he predicted. 'I know I'll get ridiculed, and I'm trying to prepare for it, but this is not some gimmicky scientific approach. I don't want people to think it's flashy; there's a reason for everything in my food.'

In 2003, during a trip to Denmark, Blumenthal made a significant progression in the creation of what has become one of his most celebrated dishes. He was in the country to demonstrate his liquid nitrogen method of producing ice cream for a major enzyme producer. Ice cream could be made incredibly quickly using the technique, taking a matter of seconds, rather than minutes or hours. This speedy method also meant that ice crystals did not form, giving the finished product a wonderfully creamy texture and a somewhat lumpy exterior. While they were working in Denmark, one of Blumenthal's team turned to the chef and remarked that the finished product resembled scrambled egg.

The connection between ice cream and the taste of egg was something that had been playing on Blumenthal's mind for some time. While experimenting with ways to create ice cream, he had come across a way of producing it with a definite egg flavour. Once more, he was transported to his childhood when his mother would serve him egg soldiers – boiled egg with thin slices of toast to dip into the egg – while he recuperated from an illness. In the Blumenthal household, eggs and bacon were one of the treats he had while growing up. Everything about egg spoke to the adult Blumenthal of comfort: either as he emerged from a period of illness or was rewarded for some good behaviour.

That was the inspiration for egg and bacon ice cream at The Fat Duck. The dish comprised a single spoonful of the ice cream and provoked strong reactions in its consumers, while also having the effect of cementing his reputation in the public imagination. However, this initial incarnation of the egg and bacon ice cream proved to be merely the first step in its evolution. With the comment about liquid nitrogen's effect on the appearance of ice cream, Blumenthal decided to really run with the idea and create a dish that gave full rein to his imagination. The food would be cooked at the table, with a smoke effect and a sizzling sound to add to the breakfasty vibe of the experience. Recalling childhood family holidays at the Seacroft Hotel in Cornwall where the breakfast table would include mini-cereal packets from the Kellogg's Variety Pack, he produced a Fat Duck packet to complement the food, along with Fat Duck egg boxes.

It was a marvellous experience for diners who would sit, initially aghast, as the dish was prepared in front of them. The attention to detail that Blumenthal and his team had created was astonishing. 'These details all add to the pleasure,' he wrote in *The Big Fat Duck Cookbook*, 'treading a fine line between the real and the surreal in a way that somehow makes sense.' This was a sentiment that could be a mission statement for Blumenthal's entire career.

Indeed, his eccentric ice cream flavours have become well known. Another one was red cabbage gazpacho with pommery grain mustard ice cream, a combination of ingredients that only Blumenthal could put together. Its origin came in a memory he had of drinking raw red-cabbage juice and being told that the pepper taste of it came from mustard oil. So it was that he began to experiment with variations on the theme of combining the two ingredients.

He began with the very basics. To test whether cabbage and mustard actually were complementary flavours, he simply put some cabbage leaves in his mouth and added a spoonful of mustard. The results were pleasing enough for him to set to work on the gazpacho element, which originally included red peppers but went on to be based on tomatoes. 'Topping this with a rocher of mustard ice cream might seem odd,' he concedes in *The Big Fat Duck Cookbook*, 'but it felt logical at the time.' He had been working on non-sweet ice creams for some time and was excited to see how mustard responded to being iced. Very well, discovered Blumenthal the intrepid innovator. He added red wine mayonnaise and cucumber squares to the mix and the dish was complete.

This is one of the few dishes Blumenthal has created which did not change once it was on the tasting menu. He was so pleased with it that he kept it as it was. But even so, Matthew Fort commented that the dish seemed to improve each time he tried it. Blumenthal wondered how this could be true, as everything involved in its production remained static. He concluded that what had left Fort to feel this way was that the first time he had eaten it he had been distracted by the fact the gazpacho was purple, an uncommon colour for food. However, believes Blumenthal, as Fort tried it on subsequent visits to The Fat Duck, he was no longer surprised at the purple colouring, meaning he was naturally concentrating more on the information from his other senses from the dish and was able to enjoy it more.

When Blumenthal made a presentation at the Royal Institution's Ice Cream Sunday event, he was inspired by what he learned about a woman called Agnes Bertha Marshall. Not unlike a female Victorian-era Heston Blumenthal, Marshall introduced the ice cream cone to the British public and also toyed with the idea of making ice cream at the dining table using liquid gas. Like Blumenthal, she spoke at events and gave demonstrations, becoming quite the celebrity. Blumenthal created a dish called Mrs Marshall's Margaret Cornet, using ginger water ice and apple ice cream. Although the finished product was not as sweet as ice creams in the Victorian era would have been, he was pleased with his 21st-century tribute to this 19th-century ice cream guru. Ice cream formed part of another dish later added to The Fat Duck line-up – Cox's apple with fromage blanc, apple milk caramel and vanilla ice cream.

Then there was carrot and orange lolly, which came about

as a result of a puree which Blumenthal made in 2002. He later added a candied beetroot and grapefruit lolly to the menu. It was often that Blumenthal had the most fun with his sweet dishes. His hero Nicholas Kurti had aerated meringues using a desiccator. Blumenthal decided to try the same trick with chocolate – he was about to create a dish with chocolate that had bubbles filled with the odour of mandarin. It was only after he had started serving the dish at The Fat Duck that Blumenthal noticed that the combination of the two ingredients was similar to that of Jaffa Cake biscuits, so he accordingly introduced some mandarin jelly to the recipe to make the combination more explicit.

But one more experiment into ice cream remained just that – an experiment. In 2005, he visited Monell Chemical Senses Center in Philadelphia, America. There he was shown the results of some experiments into smell involving vanilla and cinnamon. On returning home, he adapted the results of the experiments to involve taste, using ice cream. It became a very complex process which involved him commissioning design teams to produce scent bottles and straws. However, he failed to refine the process to one that could be workably reproduced in his kitchen.

Undaunted, his research continued. Salmon and liquorice are not two ingredients that most people would consider putting together, but, as we have seen, Blumenthal is not like most people. Bookworm Blumenthal was poring over the pages of a culinary tome when he discovered that asparagus and liquorice share a common compound – asparagine. He was surprised by this, as the two foodstuffs have strongly contrasting tastes. However, these are the moments that Blumenthal lives for: the chance to combine two vastly different tastes into one dish. He considered it, he has written, an 'odd couple' pairing. He tried liquorice (not something he is generally fond of) with some asparagus and was pleased with the result. However, as he later said, 'This was only a starting point.'

By happy coincidence, he was also trying to include a new seafood dish in The Fat Duck menu. Soon his mind was running riot and the end result was salmon poached in a liquorice gel – another attention-grabbing signature Blumenthal dish. It is visually striking, with the dark liquorice coating the salmon perfectly. He served it alongside vanilla mayonnaise, Manni olive oil and black truffle. He had almost used mackerel as the fish for the recipe but found the taste of it overwhelming. So it was salmon in the final analysis and the dish was added to the tasting menu in 2003. It received rave reviews from customers and grabbed the attention of the public.

Here, Blumenthal was cleverly playing on cravings, according to Dr Peter Barham, who worked with the chef on the dish. 'If you crave food, it is yearning for a sensation, not a taste, that you remember from another time, usually childhood,' he explained. 'Sweets because they made you feel good when you were sad, or maybe it was the hot chocolate you had after a long winter's walk with your mum and dad. This goes to the heart of what craving a particular food is about. When you have a craving, what you really want is that sensation in your mouth and the experience that goes with it,' he added. 'There is no such thing as being born with a sweet tooth. As a rule people who were given sweets regularly as a child – or in specific situations – will want to recreate that as adults.'

Which brings us to the pine sherbet fountain. Here, Blumenthal has written, he was trying to find a way to make the taste of fir make sense in a food environment. He had arrived at this dilemma via a typically Blumenthal-esque route involving discussions about what is contained in the tears of alligators and the sensation of sniffing the stone of a mango. All in a day's work for this man. He eventually decided that associating the fir aroma with a strong food memory would make the process work. He originally represented the sherbet fountain less than literally, in a glass with a strip of vanilla to scoop up the contents. However, he soon decided to go the whole way and designed his own version of the classic Bassett's sherbet fountain packaging. This was given as a 'pre-hit' prior to the serving of mango and Douglas fir puree.

With his reputation rocketing, Blumenthal inevitably received invitations to become involved in other restaurants. One offer he took up came from a regular diner at The Fat Duck, a businessman called Alfred Hitchcock, who had opened a restaurant called the Riverside Brasserie in Bray Marina with the music mogul Vince Power. Despite a beautiful location, and the exciting opportunity for customers to arrive by boat, it had enjoyed a quiet, modest start and Power moved on. The man Hitchcock approached to join him in the ownership stakes was a wise choice. Lee Dixon enjoyed a distinguished football career most notably for Arsenal, where he was a part of numerous successes including league titles and the 1994 European Cup Winners' Cup final victory over Parma. He was part of a revered back-four that was completed by Nigel Winterburn, Steve Bould and captain Tony Adams. Away from the game, he has long been a man with an eye on culinary business ventures. He also co-owned a Balti restaurant in the Midlands called Shimla Pinks.

The manager who guided Dixon and his team-mates to some of those latter triumphs was Frenchman Arsene Wenger – definitely a man with parallels to Blumenthal. Both are focused men who are driven by and obsessed with their work. Wenger has often been known as 'The Professor', thanks to the scientific approach he takes to training. It is not just the outdoor activities of his players that Wenger focuses on: he has also revolutionised the diets of footballers. And yet, despite all this, he remains popular among everyday people: football fans. He and Blumenthal have plenty in common.

With Dixon on board, Hitchcock approached Blumenthal to become head chef. Arsenal fan Blumenthal jumped at the chance to get involved, but chose to become the third partner in the business. It was not quite as exciting as lining up alongside Dixon on the Highbury turf, but the inclusion of a Gunners legend certainly gave the project an extra frisson of excitement for Blumenthal, who had always retained a childlike sense of wonder. He hit it off with Dixon and he counts the former Arsenal star – now a television commentator – as a valued friend.

Unfortunately, their professional relationship did not yield such a positive outcome. The early signs were positive, with the newspapers heaping praise on the relaunched venture. Blumenthal could not help but smile at two particular write-ups which included amusing passages. The *Observer*'s Jay Rayner drew a live musical analogy to sum up his enthusiasm, saying he felt like throwing his underwear at the chef, so impressed was he by food which included braised belly of pork with chorizo and borlotti beans. The *Independent*'s reviewer served up an even more pleasing comparison for Blumenthal the football fan: 'Like his Arsenal team-mate, Heston Blumenthal has done the double.'

Describing the venue, the same newspaper reported, 'This marina is not exactly Monte Carlo and nor is this casual brasserie as high-falutin' as its Michelin-starred big brother, The Fat Duck. But molecular gastronomer Heston Blumenthal's second restaurant is a hit with locals and day-trippers, with its great food (roast gilt-head bream and escabeche of red mullet) and a duck's eye view of the Thames from the decked terrace.'

Fellow broadsheet the *Daily Telegraph* also visited and offered vivid descriptions to its readers of the place. 'Outside, a fresh wind makes the Union flag on top of the flagpole strain against its leash and shakes the bare branches of the riverbank trees. The sun shines, the snowdrops dance and the only traffic on the Thames is a solitary duck, somewhat alarmed to find itself being whisked along by the fast-flowing current. Outside, there is a fabulous 60-seat deck area, while the inside has the slightly jerry-built air of a school sports pavilion or a seaside cafe – despite the modish wood panelling, the matching curved chairs and deluxe basics such as snowy linens and covetable Bernardaud crockery.'

Here, it was evident, was a writer who was not an out-and-out fan of Blumenthal and his work. This much was evident from his assertion that 'fawned over to a suffocatingly-oleaginous degree by much of the foodie press, Blumenthal is noted for his headline-friendly work in applying scientific techniques to his experiments with flavour and texture. To this end, he recently informed a catering magazine that he was creating a sardines-on-toast-flavoured ice cream. Barf.' But if it was clear that this was one writer who Blumenthal's Riverside Brasserie would have to work hard to impress – it did. 'In all, it's an incredibly impressive display of every culinary skill you can think of, served up in what is little more than an elegant shack on the banks of the Thames,' continued the writer. 'It reminds me a little of the old Gavvers restaurant in Chelsea, where the Roux brothers used to train their staff before they worked at Le Gavroche, although none of the talented kitchen crew seemed in much need of tuition.'

And, just as many of Blumenthal's dishes had a final flavour twist, the *Telegraph* review also had a sting in the tail. 'Who knows what Blumenthal has planned here for the future, but it is unlikely to remain so small or so inexpensive or so charming forever,' concluded the article.

So what went wrong? Perhaps Blumenthal's involvement had been both a blessing and a curse. Some customers seemed to view the Riverside Brasserie as an affordable version of The Fat Duck. This expectation put pressure on the venture. It was a difficult balance: how to make financially viable such a small restaurant (it had only eight tables in its dining room) where customers were not inclined to come and go quickly, making a lucrative double-sitting difficult in the evening.

But, when Blumenthal parted company with the venture in the summer of 2004, it was on good terms with his former partners, who he has since praised for their subsequent improvements to the venue's running. As he wrote in *The Big Fat Duck Cookbook*, 'It is now deservedly doing better without me.'

As he surrendered interest in the Riverside Brasserie, Blumenthal bought a new venue with a fresh venture in mind. The Hinds Head was literally on his doorstep, right next door to The Fat Duck. He had almost, at the last minute, passed up the chance to purchase The Hinds Head but his instinct pushed him on. It proved a wise investment. It had a rich history, built in the 1600s and always a right royal venue, visited once by the Queen and Duke of Edinburgh. The couple felt that it would 'be forever England'. It was also, astonishingly, the venue Blumenthal's hero Nicholas Kurti chose for his honeymoon. With such a historical feel about it, Blumenthal felt The Hinds Head was a good place for him to experiment with more old dishes and recipes. The press quickly sniffed this scent, with one reviewer writing, 'A historic meal, we declare and it's a big hit, too. Is this the start of a new retro-food fad? One small step back in time could mean many steps forward for mankind. Or at least for the people of Bray, who have at last got a place to have a decent quiet pie and a pint.'

As for Blumenthal, he at least had the space to spread out the work of himself and his colleagues. He could now use the space that his new venue afforded him to create two new kitchens and locate his staff more comfortably.

The many developments for Blumenthal in 2004 had contributed to making him an increasingly famous man. For the *Independent*, it was enough to name him one of the next big things for 2005, chiming, 'Heston Blumenthal, Britain's newest superchef, has just taken over a pub in Bray, The Hinds Head, where he intends to serve potted shrimps, pea and ham soup and treacle tart.'

CHAPTER FOUR

BENEFIT OF HINDS SIGHT

The history of what was once known as The Hinds Head Hotel is long and distinguished. As the official website for the venue says, 'The Hinds Head was built in the 15th century. Though its original purpose is unknown, some say it was a royal hunting lodge and others a guesthouse for the Abbot of Cirencester. Whatever its origins, it has been at the very heart of life in Bray as a welcoming and much-loved local pub for over 400 years.' After recounting the royal visit, it goes on to describe 'other notable visitors', such as 'King Hussein of Jordan, Errol Flynn, Walt Disney and the wife of Winston Churchill. And, of course, one famous guest – of 400 years ago – was the renowned Vicar of Bray who changed his religious allegiances several times during the religious upheavals of the 16th century in order to stay in office in his beloved Bray. A plaque commemorating him still hangs in the pub.'

As for what Blumenthal would be doing there, that was

clear from the venue's mission statement which announced, 'Working with food historians, including the team from the Tudor kitchens at Hampton Court Palace, Heston Blumenthal is rediscovering the delights of our culinary past and bringing long-forgotten British dishes such as powdered goose, mutton ham and quaking pudding back onto the menu.'

'In researching dishes for The Hinds Head, we've come up with some really interesting old stuff,' added Blumenthal. 'There are so many recipes from the past that have been forgotten. We should be bringing those back and developing them in a modern context. Some of the recipes appear rather crude and I wouldn't suggest preparing them in the same way as in the past, but it's possible to develop them using up-to-date techniques. It makes sense to revive some of our great, buried dishes from the past and modernise them, rather than always trying to reinvent the wheel.'

It sounded a fascinating prospect, but what of the venue in which it would be served?

Inside, the history of the venue is clear to visitors. A *Daily Telegraph* journalist describes it thus: 'The Hinds Head is the sort of boozer every good village deserves. With plenty of wood panelling, a big open inglenook fireplace and loads of cosy alcoves, it has a hearty atmosphere, steeped in history.'

As with the Riverside Brasserie, one of the challenges for The Hinds Head was to emerge from the shadows of the success of The Fat Duck, while not being unaware of its legendary neighbour.

Writing in the *Telegraph*, journalist Belinda Richardson recalled a conversation with her sister that summed up this paradoxical challenge. She asked her sibling whether she would like to accompany her to the new Blumenthal venue. 'He's the one with all those Michelin stars who makes snail porridge and sardines on toast sorbet, isn't he?' she answered. 'No, thanks. I prefer eating food that comes from a kitchen rather than a laboratory.'

Belinda continued, 'Rumour has it he's cut the gastronomic gags and is concentrating on serving unadulterated British classics instead.'

Her sibling's response showed just how much Blumenthal's eccentricity had seeped into the public imagination. 'Blimey,' said her sister. 'That sounds even more dangerous. Imagine the sort of Willy Wonka tricks he'll play on the likes of sausages and mash. What's he serving? Everlasting pork scratchings or a ploughman's that glows in the dark? Don't tell me the wallpaper's lickable, too?'

Visitors were soon coming from far and wide to test out the food at The Hinds Head – and they were liking what they found. *Time* magazine's reviewer cited Robert May's 1660 book *The Accomplisht Cook* as an influence on the restaurant when he reported that Blumenthal had been 'peppering The Hind's Head's menu with dishes that reach back to the roots of British cuisine. It can be a challenge: May's measurements include "a small bigness" and "as much flour as will lie on a shilling." But when the finished product hits the table, the taste seems worth the centuries-long wait. The quaking pudding, a light, set-milk dessert, probably hasn't wobbled this deliciously since King Charles II beckoned Nell Gwynne to try a spoonful.'

Blumenthal also entertained some guests from a Pittsburgh newspaper. 'Of course, despite its name, The Hinds Head hasn't been a hotel for 50 years,' he told them. 'Also, over time it lost its reputation for fine food and wine. Still, it's the village pub – and really important to the community.'

A visitor from closer to home was *The Times* restaurant critic Michael Winner. The well-known writer noted that there were witty sayings peppered around the walls of The Hinds Head. 'Fear knocked at the door. Faith answered. No-one was there,' was one such saying. On the way to the toilet, over a low ceiling, there was another that read: 'Caution – duck or grouse'. Winner did not approve of these and recommended they be removed hastily. However, of the rest of his experience he was incredibly positive. 'I first visited his Fat Duck restaurant in Bray in Berkshire when Heston had no stars,' he wrote. 'He was, and is, a chef of outstanding skill. He's also the only sane chef I've met. Even though you might wonder, when, on my last visit, a waiter appeared with a teaspoon, instructed me to open my mouth and then stuffed the contents in.'

So, in Winner, Blumenthal had a confirmed fan. Perhaps the eccentric writer admired Blumenthal's oddities as well as his food. Having charmed him at The Fat Duck, could the chef woo the writer under a new roof? 'Heston whiles away his time delving into ever more fanciful experiments while the other Michelin-starred chef in Bray, Michel Roux, turns out boring and dreary food at his Waterside Inn,' wrote Winner. Of The Hinds Head, he purred, 'There they serve the best pub food in the world. It's spectacularly simple. It's spectacularly good. This is the sort of restaurant I dream of finding but, even though I'm in my dotage, have never found before.' He was particularly impressed by the triple-cooked chips, which he described as 'Super-stratospheric incredible. One of the greatest tastes in the history of the world.' Overall, he concluded, The Hinds Head was 'close to perfect', adding, 'Perfect, in case you're wondering, is above historic. Flock to The Hinds Head, anyway. You'll love it. If you don't, sue me. See if I care.'

There are no records of anyone suing Winner as a result of a visit to The Hinds Head, but one *Times* reader did write to the newspaper to complain about a visit they had: 'At Heston Blumenthal's Hinds Head, Bray, we ordered a bottle of wine,' wrote Carolyn Dolling of Buckinghamshire. 'Two glasses came instead. Begrudgingly the glasses were removed. When our bottle of wine finally arrived it was already open. We asked why and were arrogantly informed: "That's the way we do it here." Certain staff members should go to charm school.'

A more positive response is provided by Jonathan Sacerdoti, interviewed for this book. 'I went to The Hinds Head for a friend's birthday,' he said, 'he'd been to The Fat Duck and actually said he preferred the pub to the main restaurant, which he had loved. I've never eaten in The Fat Duck. The ambience was not at all how I expected it to be. The pub is a lovely, traditional pub building, with wooden beams everywhere. I had expected it to be very posh and out of keeping with the area, especially as Heston is so famous throughout the world for his radical cookery style. But actually the pub seems to act as a balance for the more unusual restaurant next door: the decor and food were simple and traditional. Of course the regular gastro-pub dishes on the menu all had a great "Heston' twist".

'We were all impressed to see Heston walk through the restaurant while we were there for our lunch. It wasn't a showy display, to let the clientele know he was there. He was just walking through to get downstairs. It was reassuring to know he's hands-on and works in the actual place he puts his name to, unlike some celebrity chefs. We got the sense that he was still very involved and interested in the place.'

As we have seen, for Blumenthal, service is as important as the quality of the food – if not more so. Here, Sacerdoti scores the venue highly. 'As we walked upstairs to our table, having booked, we asked how the downstairs operated. Apparently they don't take bookings for the downstairs section, which explained why it was full of people who looked like very ordinary locals, instead of out-of-towners like us who had made the trip specially to Bray to eat Heston's food. I think it's great that that is how they work. Downstairs is laid out as a regular pub might be, whereas upstairs is more like a restaurant, with a few sections and rooms so that it never feels empty even if there aren't many diners there.

'I can't remember much specifically about the food (sorry) but I do remember trying the ice cream, knowing that he makes it in a very unusual way with liquid nitrogen, and actually I didn't think it was as nice as a normal fresh egg ice cream. Sometimes I think you can mess with something too much just to be a bit clever, and miss the whole point of the "traditional" way of making it. I think traditional dishes have been through a natural evolution and reinventing them is often counterproductive, as was the case with this ice cream.'

By the time that The Hinds Head was acquired, Heston had not only a second but a third Michelin star. Speculation about the second had begun to circulate as the tasting menu evolved over the months. One person who was not taking part in the gossip was the man himself, who had certainly not expected such an honour in a hurry. So imagine his feeling on the day in 2002 when he received news of the award for The Fat Duck. Blumenthal had been driving west to Bristol for a routine meeting when the call came through. He recognised the number of The Fat Duck on the screen of his ringing mobile phone, and took the call. One of his colleagues told him that the following day he would officially be awarded the second star. He was taken aback by this astonishing news. As he tried to concentrate both on the road and on the news he had just received, his ever-focused mind turned less to emotion and more to what this meant for the running of the restaurant. He started speaking about how they would have to alter the staff line-up. His colleague had hoped to hear cheering and whooping from the boss and wondered aloud if Blumenthal could leave the practicalities to one side for a moment and simply enjoy the news.

Inside, of course, Blumenthal was delighted and proud. He enjoyed telephoning family and friends to pass on the news. If he was less than demonstrative, it was because he was alive to the challenges that a second star would immediately bring to The Fat Duck. Those challenges were to bring Blumenthal's venture to the brink of financial disaster over the following two years.

It was around then that he developed one of the recipes for which he was to become most famous: snail porridge. The inspiration for this dish owes itself to a coincidence of two events on the same day. A delivery of snails arrived at The Fat Duck, the first time such a foodstuff had gone through its doors, on the same day that his head chef returned from a holiday in New York. Blumenthal immediately asked his colleague where he had eaten in Manhattan, a city rich in fine restaurants. He was initially disappointed to learn that his head chef had patronised a Chinese restaurant. Unimaginative, thought Blumenthal. Until, that is, his chef told him what he ate there: fish porridge. As he heard of this interesting combination of fish and oats, Blumenthal was making snail cannelloni. It was another eureka moment: what about snail porridge? After the customary Fat Duck investigation and experimentation, he completed and perfected a new dish. He was mindful that the idea of snail porridge might raise eyebrows among some diners, so he included ingredients that were commonly associated with snail, such as parsley and Pernod.

He enjoyed watching people being surprised by the food they ate. It was the same with his beetroot jelly. 'It's funny when you watch people eat it,' he said with excitement. 'Tell them it's beetroot and they start to look nervous and don't know if they like it. But if you say it's blackcurrant they think it's delicious. In fact, beetroot, like blackcurrant, contains tartaric acid and that's what makes them taste so similar.'

The *New Scientist* described him as 'a culinary postmodernist, mixing form and content, appearance and flavour', and quoted him as saying, 'I enjoy seeing how people react when they realise what they are eating is not what they thought. I want diners to be pulled out of their food comfort zone.'

But, as 2004 dawned, The Fat Duck found itself in a perilous situation. Despite a host of new dishes being introduced to the tasting menu, The Fat Duck was often scarcely populated. Then, one day as he pored over the depressing reading that was his accounts book, Blumenthal made a terrifying discovery: he would not be able to pay his staff their wages which were due at the end of the week. He later recalled, 'I was two days away from going under. I didn't have enough cash to pay the wages and my wife didn't know. I had two Michelin stars and top scores from all the guidebooks and yet I was nearly bankrupt.'

Salvation would come at the last minute and when Blumenthal was least expecting it – in fact, it would arrive when he wasn't even in the country. He had received a very exciting invitation to the Madrid Fusion conference. This was a glorious, annual get-together for the culinary world.

The biggest names in the chef and food critic trade descend on the Palacio Municipal de Congresos for it. Blumenthal was delighted to be asked to attend having read all about the event in his beloved books all those years earlier. Now, he was being asked to attend. Thrilling. Only it got better than that – Heston had also been given the chance to give a presentation, including such subjects as cooking with liquid nitrogen and with high and low pressure. He would perform in front of the assembled gastronomic royalty, listed alongside internationally renowned heavyweight gastronomics. As the *Boston Globe* reported, 'Fusion was to feature the lions of the new cuisine: Ferran Adrià from El Bulli, Juan Mari Arzak from Arzak in San Sebastian and Heston Blumenthal from The Fat Duck outside London.'

To say the occasion made Blumenthal anxious would be an understatement: he was wracked with images of the audience walking out of the room before he had completed his presentation – those chefs who were his heroes, the men whose example had made him decide to take up the trade in the first place.

This was not the first time that Blumenthal had given a presentation to a live audience and on the previous occasion he had also spoken in front of at least one of his heroes. In 2001, he had been invited to the Erice Workshop on Molecular and Physical Gastronomy. An annual event since its inception in 1992, Erice was a conference where the scientific side of cooking was expertly discussed. It was put together by the triumvirate of Nicholas Kurti, Harold McGee and Herve This.

On his way to the 2001 Sicily conference, Blumenthal was introduced to McGee, one of his all-time heroes. He got up and spoke about flavour issues to a room full of scientists and chefs. His speech was enjoyed by the audience and a healthy discussion followed. Professor Barham was one of those attending: 'We try to get chefs to pose questions that we can answer,' he said. 'Heston is the perfect chef from our point of view. He has an open mind. He actually uses the research, whereas most chefs pick up the bits that reinforce their preconceptions and just ignore the rest.'

Tamsin Day-Lewis was another person impressed by his contribution: 'Having witnessed the seriousness which the physicists, food scientists, chefs and writers afforded Heston's theories – and his wit – at the Molecular Gastronomy workshop in Sicily last month. From my point of view, anyone who keeps asking questions and searching for answers that make kitchen life easier and more delicious and is prepared to share the new-found knowledge can only be a kindred spirit.

Could he similarly woo people at Madrid Fusion? He put together as impressive a presentation as he could muster and flew club class – his first taste of such a luxury – to the Spanish capital. Waiting for him at the airport was Spanish wine expert Javier Zaccagnini. Blumenthal was ushered to his impressive BMW car and they whizzed off to the hotel together. In his suite was a gift from his hosts: a posh, leather document holder. Back home, his life was a precarious, frenetic affair, so he enjoyed being pampered by the organisers with his posh plane tickets and fine accommodation. He remained nervous about his presentation but needn't have done. Although he spoke quickly at first in front of the assembled mass of 800 people, all went to plan – including an audacious final flourish when he invited each member of the audience to inflate and let off balloons scented with marzipan to produce a climax of multi-sensory drama. It was, as he was painfully aware, a stunt with plentiful potential to backfire. As the balloons flew into the air and then sank to the floor, his presentation concluded. It had been fantastic, supported by graphics from the *Kitchen Chemistry* show. Michel Roux rushed to the stage and took Blumenthal's microphone from him. He told the assembled masses that he was proud of Blumenthal, who he saw as his son. The Brit was then mobbed by the media, all keen to speak to this rising star of the gastronomic globe, who shone brighter than ever before in the Spanish capital in front of his heroes.

The remainder of his time in Madrid was a triumphant experience for Blumenthal. The day after his presentation, he rushed from meeting to interview, still on a high from the success of his award. He had also received word from home that The Fat Duck had received another honour. The *Observer Food Monthly* had named Blumenthal's pride and joy the Best Restaurant in its annual poll. This was an award that was voted for not by specialists or experts, but rather it came from the readers. It was therefore a great shot in the arm for Blumenthal. Together with the rapturous reception his presentation had received, he was able to forget about the financial problems back at home and enjoy the taste of success. However, he was about to receive some news that would send his spirits soaring ever higher. Life was about to change dramatically for The Fat Duck owner.

As he prepared to go for lunch on the second day of Madrid Fusion, Blumenthal received two phone calls in swift succession. The message of both callers was the same: to tell him that The Fat Duck was about to receive its third Michelin star. The first call came from the restaurant when the story remained nothing more than an unconfirmed rumour. It was only when one of the editors of the *Michelin Guide* called that Blumenthal could finally allow himself to believe that the speculation was based in fact. He immediately called his wife whose joy was loud and fulsome. 'Another week and we would completely have run out of money,' he said. 'I couldn't even pay the wages. I remember calling her with the news and her screaming, just screaming at the other end of the telephone, with joy.' True, they were still experiencing financial difficulties. True, The Fat Duck was still often semi-deserted on weekdays (the day the third star was awarded only two tables were occupied for dinner). However, this third star was a rope to the business as they struggled to keep it afloat. This was to bring him increased fame and recognition; surely they would soon be in calmer waters?

The award marked an interesting development not just for Blumenthal but for perceptions of the Michelin awarding process itself. The Fat Duck undoubtedly served fine food but its interior was not what could be described as exceptionally luxurious. Therefore, the awarding of a third star to it helped to alter the public perception of what it took to receive the award. It really was about the food, not the luxury. Restaurant surroundings were marked by a separate set of Michelin criteria – a symbol of a knife and fork. Marks would be awarded out of five in this regard and The Fat Duck received a mark of two for this category. Blumenthal was not crestfallen by this news: instead he felt that the contrast between the exceptional luxurious food and more everyday interior gave his restaurant a character he was proud of.

A comedic moment soon after the award showed the contrast perfectly. Two of the Michelin judges visited The Fat Duck to talk over the implications of its third star with Blumenthal. They also reassured the owner that, as long as he continued cooking as he was, he would not lose the third star. They urged him not to change his overall approach. One of them was midway through explaining to Blumenthal that stars were awarded for quality of food and not the level of luxury in the restaurant itself when two workers came through the dining room, dragging large, smelly wheelie bins in their wake.

Before he could get down to exploiting the work that the third star would create, Blumenthal had lots of celebrating to do. He'd made a start while he was still in Madrid. Surrounded by his peers, Blumenthal basked in rays of glory. Nobu Matsuhisa gave his demonstration and during it he made the announcement to the conference audience that The Fat Duck had just received its third Michelin star. The audience rose to their feet to acclaim the British chef.

He received a second standing ovation later in the day as he dined in a nearby restaurant. The celebrating continued into the early hours when Blumenthal found himself being 'blessed' with a dab of champagne on to his head at 2am.

He also had an interview with four journalists to attend the next day. It had been pre-scheduled and the scribes got a bigger scoop than they bargained for as their star interviewee sat down and blurted out the news from Bray. Naturally, they bombarded him with questions about this. Here he received a lesson in media relations. He joked that his parents christened him Heston because they were such fans of the food at Heston service station. When he woke up the following day to see his comment reported on the front page of British newspapers as fact he was horrified, but not half as much as his parents who took months to forgive him.

'When I flew back, there were stories on BBC news and a headline in *The Times* saying, "Chef named after parents' love of motorway service station gains third star",' he recalled. 'I spent six months apologising to them.' He's still not sure how his parents came up with the name. 'I'd asked my parents where my name came from, but they never gave a clear answer. They said, "Oh, it's just a name."'

He returned on a Friday evening and found a monument to his success had been assembled by his wife and kids. 'I walked into the living room and Zanna had cut out the front page of *The Times* – [mass murderer] Harold Shipman was in the margin –' a splutter of laughter '– and that was in a frame with three balloons blown up and gold stars and cards, which made me shed a tear. My family were all asleep. I poured myself a glass of wine and just sat there and there are very, very few times when I wake up and smell the roses and I don't know if I said it at the time, but I thought, It's all been worth it.'

Along with the excitement of the third star came an increased sense of responsibility in Blumenthal. He shook up The Fat Duck and made it a more slick operation. Longstanding problems such as the uneven tables were addressed, new staff were appointed to work on the administration and structure of the operation, and air-conditioning was introduced. After a period of anxiety over his own performance post-three stars, Blumenthal eventually relaxed and continued doing what he does best: experimenting and pushing the boundaries of food preparation. With the additional kitchens in The Hinds Head, he had more space and time to work on new ideas. Previously, he had been forced to perform all his experimentation in the cramped Fat Duck kitchen or – to the occasional consternation of his wife – at home in their kitchen. He had also previously been forced to do most of his work on Mondays, the day that The Fat Duck did not open.

With the third star in place, Blumenthal felt empowered to spend more time pursuing the course that really fired up his imagination: investigating the links between the brain and food. He was very surprised by the award. 'I thought one day I'd maybe have a place with a Michelin star,' he said. 'I never thought I'd have two and I certainly never thought or had an ambition for three. Whether or not you believe in the *Michelin Guide*, whether you think it's right or wrong, the fact is that after you get three stars the phone starts ringing and suddenly the CVs start to come through from talented staff who want to work for you. There's no other guide that has as much impact on your business in that way.'

Meantime, Blumenthal had been sharpening not just his knives but also his pen as he wrote his first book. *Family Food* was a book that continued to show the world what Blumenthal's approach was all about, but also showed that he retained the common touch. He recalled that many were surprised that for his first book he decided to write a book that encouraged parents to involve children in their cooking. However, he believed it was perfectly consistent with his approach of presenting what he learned in the most approachable form possible. What better and more accessible way was there to achieve this than to produce a family book which aimed to appeal to all, young and old alike? Furthermore, there has always been an almost childlike wonder to Blumenthal's work so he was not destined to have to try hard to make his work appealing and understandable to the younger generation.

He had first embarked on the project at the behest of his friend Nick Wilson, who knew a thing or two about culinary publishing, having worked for giants Penguin on cookery titles. It was to that publisher that Blumenthal sold his book. It was four years in the making: he started writing it in 1998 and it didn't hit the shelves until 2002. He was as meticulous in his writing as he was his cooking.

For three years, he refined, revised and polished his work as new ideas occurred to him. *Family Food* was a book written in the hours of darkness. Having worked all day and much of the evening at The Fat Duck, Blumenthal would rush home and write.

Of course, writing this book gave Blumenthal yet another excuse to do what he loved to do: to almost drown himself in books about food. He swam through libraries of classic and obscure books about culinary history, and made some surprising discoveries. 'I came across a manuscript from Taillevent, who was a chef to the Palais Royal in Paris in about 1300,' he explains. 'There was a recipe where you plucked a chicken while it was still alive, and then brushed its skin with wheat germ and saffron and dripping and then you put the head under the belly and rocked it to sleep. You put it on the serving platter with two roasted chickens and then started carving one of the roast chickens at the table. While you were carving, the chicken that was asleep would wake up and squawk and run across the table.' There's an idea, he thought, storing the concept away for the future. However, he was horrified by a similar discovery involving a goose.

'The most disturbing recipe I've ever seen is for "how to roast a goose alive" from *The Cook's Oracle* from the late 1800s,' he said. 'It's written almost in biblical style and it's really disturbing. The idea is that you've cooked the goose's skin but the vital organs are still working and you carve the goose while it can still scream. You just don't know if anyone ever actually made that dish – not that it's one I'd specifically like to see. But I would like to go back to see some of the creativity. There was a lot of stuff going on 300 years ago and that, for me, is really fascinating.'

The introduction to *Family Food* is a lengthy and passionate call to arms. Here is the Blumenthal manifesto unashamedly spelled out for all to read. He rails against the 'gimmick'-ridden nature of some previous cookbooks aimed at children. He also bemoans the power of the supermarkets with their enticingly packaged processed food aimed at the young. He recalls sheepishly returning from a visit to a supermarket with his two daughters, and his wife admonishing him for falling for all the requests the girls had made of him. He mourns the 'disintegration of local communities' that the power of supermarket chains has wrought. The mission element comes across again as he writes of 'poor-quality produce, substandard family restaurants, media misinformation' and explains that he wants to 'empower' readers and fill them with 'confidence'. Here, perhaps for the first time, the passion and ambition of Blumenthal was displayed for all to see. He predicted boldly that 'the world of cooking and eating will not be the same again'.

He also explained how taste works alongside other senses. To explain this, he suggested a fun test for parents and children to do together. A volunteer would be blindfolded and have their nostrils pushed together. They would then be invited to drink through a straw from four glasses which contained fizzy orange, cola, lemonade and tonic water. He predicted that the only drink they would be likely to identify would be the tonic water, due to its bitterness. This eccentric exercise, he explained, was a great way to show children – and adults in all likelihood – the difference between taste and flavour. He explained to the readers that he had employed a similar method to convince his children to eat peppered food. They had always been against it, but he then asked them to sample beef with and then without the seasoning. They were quickly won round, he was pleased to say.

Following the introduction, he presented a series of recipes under the headings: snacks, grains, soups, Sunday lunch, vegetables, fish and desserts. For each recipe he included a boxed-off 'children's tip', to bring them into the process.

The book received a lot of praise from reviewers. 'Heston Blumenthal is a genuinely talented chef, both intuitive and innovative in the kitchen,' began the *Time Out* magazine review. 'To its credit *Family Food* offers tastes and techniques that children will find very exciting. His recipes work, some with thrillingly simple ease... *Family Food* is a treasure trove of useful dishes, sensibly and sensitively explained.' *The Times* described it as 'a welcome antidote to the funny-face school of cookery' and the *Daily Mirror* confirmed its appeal to children saying it was 'an eye-opening approach to what little angels should eat'.

But was it a book that appealed to anyone other than children? Fellow chef Anthony Worrall Thompson certainly thought so. 'This is a book to get all the family cooking,' he advocated. 'Heston is a genius... it provides us with great

Above: The Fat Duck…

Below: … and Heston with the tasting menu in action.

Blumenthal at the British Academy Television Awards.

Influences on Heston include, *above left*, Graham Kerr, the 'galloping gourmet' and, *above right*, American expert Harold McGee. Fellow ace chefs include, *below left*, Marco Pierre White and, *below right*, Le Manoir aux Quat'Saisons supremo Raymond Blanc.

Above left: Heston at the launch of *The Big Fat Duck Cookbook*.

*Above righ*t: Blumenthal and Zanna out in 2008.

Below: The Mandarin Oriental Hotel, home of Foliage, the restaurant that Heston had been linked to.

Above: The Queen looks less than convinced at the prospect of ice cream cooked with liquid nitrogen...

Below left: ...though Prince Phillip looks more intrigued.

Below right: Peter Barham worked on *Kitchen Chemistry* with Blumenthal.

Above: With Gary Lineker and Emma Rushin, who won the competition to find a new flavour of crisps.

Below: The Little Chef at Popham attained legendary status once it featured in Heston's show.

With Ferran Adrià at the awards for the world's 50 best restaurants in 2008.

Heston attends Buckingham Palace to receive his OBE.

recipes we can all get involved with.' This was exactly what the author had aimed for.

The *Observer* joined in the love fest, saying, '*Family Food* bears the hallmark of [Blumenthal's] thoughtful, measured and quirky approach to cuisine... the recipes are interesting and easy for children.' It was not the only Sunday broadsheet to heap praise on Blumenthal's book. The *Independent on Sunday* gushed that *Family Food* was 'a sure candidate for recipe book of the year'.

Between writing and cooking and developing, it was a busy life for Blumenthal, but he was in love with his work. And he had to be, because, as he knew, the only way to make a restaurant work is to put in a huge amount of hours. He would routinely rise at 5am and it would be common for him to still be working at 2am the following morning. In between, he would have occasional brief sleeps, using a gathering of dirty laundry as a makeshift bed. His exhaustion was easy to spot in his appearance and, at times, behaviour. On one occasion he fell asleep while trimming a fish and on another attempted to light a blowtorch by holding it under a flowing tap. But, if nothing else, the song 'I Don't Like Mondays' didn't apply to Blumenthal in these days, as it was the only day of the week that allowed him to sleep in. His body grabbed the chance to refuel with extended slumber.

These were tough times not just for Blumenthal but his family. He and his wife had invested every penny they had into making The Fat Duck and now The Hinds Head work. He was driving a £100 car and then a £150 Metro with a ridiculously bad paint job. Finding the time and money to look after their two children was a huge challenge. They were forever in Heston's thoughts, not least when a faulty boiler in a home they were renting led to his having to have both Jack and Jessica tested for carbon monoxide poisoning.

Customers arrived at The Hinds Head expecting more traditional pub fare. They wanted straightforward meat and two vegetables and complained about the way their food had been cooked. These people were not even happy with the relatively small level of experimentation he was performing in the kitchen. He was going to need customers with a greater sense of adventure as his project developed.

From very early on, he was producing interesting dishes such as triple-cooked chips, the results of experimenting into ways of cooking them which had been going on for two years. The triple-cooked method involved boiling them, then chilling them in a fridge then frying them twice. The result was the dream chip from his point of view: ultra-crispy on the outside but soft on the inside. He had come by this perfection on simple instinct and he was delighted with the result – the first Fat Duck dish that he could 'call my own'.

In April 2005, Blumenthal received yet further public recognition of the brilliance of his work when The Fat Duck was named best restaurant in the world by the prestigious *Restaurant* magazine. It was an astonishingly satisfying honour for Blumenthal, and he was quick to share the glory that had been bestowed upon him. 'There are so many very good chefs in the world I cannot believe my name is even in the running for the top,' he said. 'It is fantastic for Britain, though this is all down to the Roux brothers, who first put England on the gastronomic map,' he added. He said it felt 'incredible' to be considered the best in the world. The award came off the back of growing public affection. 'I continually become more surprised each time,' he said, before predicting even greater things to come from The Fat Duck. 'Whatever our ultimate goal might be, we are not there yet and it feels a bit early. Though the restaurant opened ten years ago, we still feel very young and we have much more energy to give.'

The editorial team of *Restaurant* magazine was fulsome in its praise of Blumenthal. Joe Warwick, the associate editor, said, 'There are a lot of people who don't like the food Heston is doing, but the real foodies, the chefs and critics who judged these awards, know he is pushing the boundaries and pushing food in a new direction. The award is the culmination of what has been happening to cooking in Britain since the mid-1990s and makes it now the best place to eat, especially in London and just outside. You can still get appalling food in restaurants outside London. I just don't think there is a good food culture here as there is in France and Italy. But food trends trickle down from restaurants and some time that will trickle down to people's own kitchens.'

Ella Johnston, the editor, took up the theme, placing the improvement in British restaurants in its context. 'British chefs used to just go abroad to the US and France,' she said. 'Now, with people becoming more adventurous eaters and with more money in London and the surrounding areas, they know they will have an audience for great food.'

With British food being so widely praised and recognised, a backlash was inevitable and came soon after the award. Wolfram Siebeck is a veteran, hugely respected food critic in Germany. Off the back of the award, he visited The Fat Duck. It's safe to say he did not enjoy what he found. 'If The Fat Duck is the best restaurant in the world, it has the worst service,' he wrote. 'In places of this quality, the guest should not have to wait more than half-an-hour for bread and wine and would prefer not to be spoken to in an incomprehensible dialect.' Once the food proper began to arrive, he was scarcely more impressed. 'When the performance finally began,' he wrote, 'the opening was a white foam of green tea from a spray can, which with the help of liquid nitrogen was transformed into a half-solid morsel. Why, I'm not sure. I prefer to drink green tea hot and in a cup.'

Siebeck was also unimpressed by the 'nut-sized dumpling' brought to him on 'two huge plates'. The dish, he grumbled, 'was supposedly mustard ice'. He then delivered a memorable image: 'With this fart of nothingness, the leitmotiv of this cuisine became clear to me. It was the old nouvelle cuisine.'

There seemed to be some national rivalry involved, which became clearer when he said, 'Where 14 English restaurants are cooking their way to Albion grandeur, our goose roasts don't have much of a chance. So again: congratulations to our English friends! What they were unable to achieve in football, they've made up for in the kitchen. This counter-balances the bankruptcy of their last car company and the state of the London underground.'

When the British press took up this story, a spokeswoman for The Fat Duck was contacted. 'It's clear that Mr Siebeck didn't really enjoy his meal with us,' she said with a fine line in English understatement.

Fortunately, others felt happier with the magazine award. Dr David Giachardi, chief executive of the Royal Society of Chemistry, said, 'We are delighted with Heston's success. His work at The Fat Duck using scientific principles to create new and exciting combinations of flavour and taste has raised the awareness of molecular gastronomy in the UK. Heston's curiosity to investigate the fundamental processes behind cooking and thereby push the boundaries of the culinary art is an inspiration. We are currently collaborating with Heston to develop an educational resource that will highlight the vital role played by chemistry in our everyday lives. Food and cooking provide an exciting context for teaching chemistry and a way to engage students with the subject.'

With another honour on his sideboard, it was time for Blumenthal to increase his fame and influence, as the BBC signed him up to front an exciting new series...

CHAPTER FIVE

IN SEARCH OF PERFECTION

In November 2005, Blumenthal went under the surgeon's knife. This was not part of a crazy Fat Duck experimentation, but a genuine operation – and a dangerous one at that. The spinal-fusion operation was a success and brought to an end what he described as decades of crippling back pain. He had been reluctant to go under the knife, but relented when the gravity of his situation was spelled out to him. 'The operation was a last resort,' he said. 'I wasn't keen but the surgeon told me, "If you don't have this operation you'll be in a wheelchair. You won't walk again."' This was news that focused Blumenthal's mind, but he had been in terrible pain for some time. He continued, 'Standing in one place and twisting from side to side makes it worse and that's exactly what you do in a kitchen,' he explained. 'I've been going to an osteopath since I was 15 and I'd been having acupuncture but it was still painful. Some days I wouldn't be able to lift my foot off the floor.'

In 2004, he had been referred to a specialist and given an MRI scan. There, after finally discovered the problem: lytic spondylolisthesis. 'The bottom bone in my back wasn't sitting on the base of the spine and it was rubbing. The sciatic nerve was trapped in a little hole.' With such a grave diagnosis and even graver prognosis, he finally agreed to have the operation, and timed it to coincide with The Fat Duck's Christmas closure. The alternative was too much to consider. 'It was possible that in 15 years the fusion might have happened on its own,' he was told. 'The bone would have worn the disc down and the spine would have fused together and repaired itself – if I could have put my feet up for 15 years. But I couldn't do nothing for 15 years. My mind would go first.'

The spinal-fusion operation was not just risky, it was complicated, too. Blumenthal, however, has his own – typically quirky – description of how it works. 'You know the little wings there are on either side of each vertebra?' he begins. 'Well, they cut them off, ground them up with some glue, packed them into a little cage where the disc should be, lifted the vertebra and bolted them together. Thursday was the first time I saw the scan after the operation and I saw all the metalwork. It looks like something you would get from Homebase. I would recommend it to anyone. It was a last resort but it's been surprisingly easy. Human beings are really adaptable and I think if you put up with anything for long enough you get used to it. I expected to feel a lot more uncomfortable after the operation but I'm all right. The hardest thing is not trying to run before I can walk.'

Around the same time, Blumenthal was given an honorary degree by Reading University. Announcing the award, Professor Donald Mottram, of the university's School of Food Biosciences, said, 'While Heston has been developing a novel approach to food at his restaurant... he has had frequent contact with the School. He visits for discussions on all sorts of aspects of food science. He and his staff also helped students on the food product development modules. He is recognised as the leading authority on molecular gastronomy, the relationship between chemical and physical properties of food and its presentation and perception by humans.'

It was another symbolic recognition of his work and came at a good time for Blumenthal. It took a few months to recuperate from the operation and then he was ready to take on his next project – a search for the ultimate in food preparation. Nothing new for him in that, you might think, except that this time he would be making the search in front of millions of viewers. He was commissioned by the BBC to present a series of programmes called *In Search of Perfection*. Acknowledging that everybody's concept of perfection is different, he spoke to numerous experts and cooks, and undertook his own research as well.

'Heston Blumenthal, the culinary pioneer whose most famous dish is snail porridge, is to join the ranks of the celebrity chefs Gordon Ramsay and Delia Smith by fronting a prime-time television series,' announced the consumer affairs correspondent of the *Independent*, Martin Hickman. 'He will apply his scientific approach to well-known dishes such as fish and chips and bangers and mash.'

Blumenthal himself said, 'It's The Fat Duck approach, but adapted to everyday dishes. We haven't necessarily gone for the most expensive ingredients but expense is not a consideration. If people can't get part of the equipment then we have found an alternative.' He accepted that perfection is an inexact concept. 'Perfection is subjective and to do with nostalgia. What's perfect for one person won't necessarily be for another,' he said. He was also characteristically honest when he admitted that one of his motivations in presenting the series was to make money. 'Margins at The Fat Duck are so tight,' he said. 'After the third Michelin star and Restaurant of the Year, I thought I wanted to get some financial security for my family without losing my integrity and hopefully this will achieve that.'

It would achieve plenty more beside, including fame, a commodity that Blumenthal would not complain about in the way that many modern-day celebrities do, 'because it brings an awful lot of benefits – and, anyway, I was the one who made the decision to appear on television,' he declared pragmatically. He says there is no need for any chef to be apologetic for putting their face on the small screen. 'There's nothing wrong. If any chef criticises a chef for going on television, then they'd better not write a cookery book.'

The series kicked off with Blumenthal searching for the perfect roast chicken and roast potato dish. On beginning his poultry quest, he found himself confronted by an enormous chicken sculpture. Made of steel and nearly four storeys high, it was quite a sight for Blumenthal to behold. He had been travelling around Lyon when he drove into a service station off the autoroute 39, a popular route. They visited the gift shop and found it a living tribute to the chicken. There, he was delighted to discover, one could buy all manner of chicken-related merchandise including T-shirts, oven gloves, tea-towels and aprons. Later, he met the area manager and noticed that his blue tie had chickens printed on it too. Everywhere he turned, Blumenthal noticed chicken photographs. He wondered if, far from overestimating the popularity of the poulet, he had in fact underestimated it.

He then queued up in L'Arche cafeteria, which turned out to be a service station not quite like any he had been to before. He found it 'homely' and 'rustic', noting that the exposed beams added to this atmosphere. There were posh cheeses on offer, along with a classy creme brulee and a selection of fine breads, including baguettes. He snapped up some bread to go with his Bresse chicken. Here, he was once more connecting with his past. He would eat roast chicken baguettes as a kid when he picnicked in Windsor Great Park. It was a regular stop en route to the park at Andrianov's delicatessen in Connaught Street. As he assembled his chicken and bread in L'Arche, he was transported back to those childhood picnics by the flavour and aromas of the food. He could have been back at those picnics, back at Andrianov's deli. It is not often, as he noted, that a motorway service station manages to be such a strong evoker of memories. He was not surprised to learn that, despite the Bresse chicken being an expensive bird, many commuters took to timing their journey so they passed L'Arche during their lunch hour.

Not only was it a glorious chicken, but, as Blumenthal noted, even its appearance made it highly suitable for the French food buff. It had blue, white and red elements which echoed the French flag. This was due to the high acid content in the soil of the region, which effectively bleached the feet of the chicken blue and made the feathers all the whiter.

Blumenthal was keen to research where the beautiful flavours came from and he visited a farm where they are reared to find out. Bon Repos is a farm in eastern France run by an award-winning man called Christian Chotard. When he arrived, he was confronted by a contrasting atmosphere. It was a tranquil setting populated by boar hunters, wearing army clothes with shotguns in their hands. Chotard, too, was dressed militarily.

Here, as at L'Arche, there was a chicken sculpture, though a far more modest affair. As ever, Blumenthal absorbed the scene in detail, his memories rich in colour. The lopsided buildings, the wisteria, geraniums and marigolds, the clusters of sweetcorn hanging from balconies. He was impressed, too, by the use of space, all of which seemed to be accounted for. Here, he learned the secrets of how the Bresse chickens get their extraordinary flavour. In this small region, the soil has little chalk which means the birds have less bone and more meat. The chickens peck away at a soil that is quite different in content to other areas. No wonder that the Bresse chickens are given special rules to live by. They live in plenty of space in the open air, Blumenthal discovered, and are given a diet of maize supplemented by wheat and milk.

Nowhere in what they eat are any hormones or chemicals. Their final weeks are spent inside so they get fatter due to decreased exercise.

Next in his search for the perfect chicken came a trip to the Les Halles food market in Lyon. Full of free tasters, the finest foods including cheese and meats were available. He had visited before many years earlier, and the place seemed to have become more modern since he was last in the area. The stalls and stores fought to capture the attention and money of passing customers. It had a bustling air that he compared to that of a middle-eastern bazaar. Here he was at home amid the flavours, colours and atmosphere. He returned to his hotel and stood on the balcony. He was staying at the Residence Des Saules hotel and from his balcony he could see the brick building that was the Restaurant Georges Blanc. The next morning, he visited Blanc's restaurant, where he would begin the next stage in his quest for the ultimate chicken, when his host would show him what he considered to be the perfect way to cook chicken. It was all great, educational stuff.

Having researched the ideal chicken, it was time for Blumenthal to look into the perfect potato. For this he travelled to the Norfolk village of Little Snoring. There, among pine trees and pheasants, was the headquarters of the potato suppliers MBM. He was amused at first by the staff's love of the spud but soon got down to taking it seriously. In the MBM boardroom, he was introduced to a hoard of potato varieties. He was at first blown away by their names: Lady Rosetta, Purple Star and even Arsey. He felt that the names – with one obvious exception – added a hint of romance to the common spud. Having examined a variety of potatoes and learned more than he could have hoped about the foodstuff, he was ready to put a shortlist of spuds to the roasting test. Which would be the ideal accompaniment to his perfect chicken? The Maris Piper potato was, for Blumenthal, the one that stood out. He was looking for the ideal combination of a crispy, crunchy outside and a pleasing, fluffy interior. He found that it had a 'glass-like' crust. The oil he used in roasting was able to enter inside of the potato and create a moist texture that further pleased Blumenthal. He had his perfect potato to complete his roast and to conclude the opening show of the series. It had been an entertaining affair.

In the next episode of the series came a push for pizza perfection. Blumenthal has always enjoyed Italian food and has long been a fan of Italian people's passionate attitude towards its preparation. He noted with admiration that a pizza association in Naples had written a code of conduct that spelled out how to make a pizza. So it was an ebullient Blumenthal who set out for Naples to begin his quest for the perfect pizza. He was not to be disappointed by the Italians. He had barely left the airport before his bus driver began to wax lyrical about why only the people of Naples knew how to cook a pizza properly, and declared that San Marzano tomatoes were key. He was not the only one to impress this advice upon Blumenthal: from expert cooks to the folk of Naples there appeared to be a culinary consensus on the importance of these tomatoes. Accordingly, Blumenthal felt he had to visit the biggest producers of tinned San Marzano tomatoes in Italy. He was followed there by Italian journalists and a member of the local government. Italians might take their food seriously but some take their public relations just as much to heart.

Between two glorious mountains lay the tomato fields where these almost mythical fruits were lovingly grown and harvested by crop-haired, darkly tanned workers. Church bells could be heard on the wind at midday, adding to the cinematic feel of the place.

Having been shown round, Blumenthal was treated to an impromptu tasting session by his hosts. They say you should never meet your heroes, but for Blumenthal it was more a case of not testing your tomatoes. He found the legendary San Marzano tomatoes pleasing in appearance but disappointing in taste. I've tasted better cherry tomatoes, he thought as he chewed. However, in due course, he would learn why the San Marzano was so prized: its low water content ensured that it did not wet the dough. Italian pizzas are cooked rapidly in very hot ovens, and therefore soggy doughs would not be given enough time to dry.

To see the cooking in action, Blumenthal visited several pizza restaurants. The first was the birthplace of the famous margherita pizza, the Pizzeria Brandi in Chiaia. The walls were lined with photographs of famous visitors, including Chelsea Clinton, daughter of Bill and Hillary. Just as the San Marzano tomatoes had disappointed him, so did the pizzas at Brandi, although he accepts that his expectations were very high.

Next on his journey was a visit to the Caputo mill, where he hoped to learn more about the basic ingredient of the dough. He was wowed by the fact that the same family had owned the mill for so many generations, a regular feature of the Italian food trade of which Blumenthal heartily approves. In the factory itself, the smell of the flour brought back memories for him of baking bread at home as a youngster. He was shown the process of making the flour and was suitably impressed. On visiting the laboratory, he was told that 'making flour for pizza is a very complex business', and by the time he left he was in no doubt that this was true. One of the best lessons he learned was that the flour for the dough must be soft; it also must not be milled to the extent that it loses all texture. This was not merely a physical consideration, but also one of taste. Suitably inspired, he took a couple of sacks of Caputo 00 flour with him to use back home in Bray.

He visited Il Pizzaiolo del Presidente, a much-recommended restaurant in Duomo, where he saw more photographs of a visiting Clinton. This time it was Bill, whose visit created such excitement that the restaurant was renamed in honour of it. Blumenthal was quickly taken by the place. He loved the atmosphere and was also impressed that there was no menu to speak of – you simply told the waiter what toppings you wanted on your pizza and that was what you got. What Blumenthal wanted more than anything was to go into the kitchen and try to learn how they were made. Here, he was thrown in at the deep end and admits that his attempts to make a circular dough and then cook it were disappointing. The finished product, he sniffed, looked less like a pizza than an unmade bed.

After a hellish encounter with Naples traffic, he was ready to visit a smaller but no less legendary pizzeria called Da Michele, which served only two types of pizza, the margherita and the marinara. Open since 1870, it was a bustling affair. Blumenthal enjoyed the pizzas he sampled and noted the all-important flavour of the dough.

Next up, he visited Enzo Coccia's Pizzeria La Notizia where pizza-making lessons were offered. Blumenthal was a keen student and his passion quickly won the approval of his teacher. There he learned just what hard work it is to hand-knead pizza dough, and was pleased to discover later that machine-kneaded dough was often tastier. He sampled countless pizza varieties produced by Enzo and nearly missed his flight home. As he was about to board that flight, Enzo arrived with samples of fine Italian food for Blumenthal to take home and a cake for his daughter, whose birthday it was that day.

With his memories, sample ingredients and lessons, Blumenthal returned to The Fat Duck kitchen to try to create the perfect pizza. First, he had to try to find a way to get the oven to the 500 degrees Celsius of Italian pizza ovens. He found that alternating between oven and grill could push the temperature up to the high 300s, which meant a pizza could be cooked as quickly as 90 seconds. True, this was not as swift as the 60 seconds it took 500-degrees ovens to cook at, but it was a huge step forward. He later thought he had bettered his initial progress when he learned that his oven reached temperatures of up to 470 degrees Celsius during the cleaning cycle. However, he was frustrated to learn, it also locked the door during such a cycle – and he couldn't open it.

He was pleased to discover that peeled tomatoes from British supermarkets could stand up admirably against the San Marzano variety, as it had never been his intention to create recipes dominated by expensive or difficult to acquire ingredients.

But it seemed not all viewers were feeling empowered to try out his imaginative cooking procedure. Writing in the *Independent*, Christopher Hirst was unconvinced: 'The whole business sounded more than a little risky to me. Having destroyed my wife's pizza stone in my first endeavour, I didn't fancy destroying our house in my second.'

Blumenthal was to return to Italy for his quest for the perfect spaghetti Bolognese. As he noted, this was something of a peculiar quest, because there is no such dish in authentic Italian cuisine. There they more commonly ate ragu sauce with tagliatelle. Before leaving, he tasted numerous types of pasta. Having tried different varieties from different suppliers, he decided that a brand called La Pasta di Aldo was the best, beating off the runner-up from Rustichella d'Abruzzo.

To make the choice, he flew out to Bologna, generally recognised as the culinary capital of Italy, and found the area to be agreeably calmer than the wildness of Naples. He visited the Antica Trattoria restaurant, where he sampled a recipe for ragu that had been developed by a woman called

Gigina Bargelesi and her daughter-in-law, and had been used for several decades. He watched enraptured as the ragu was made, noting that it was completed without stock and that it was given a slow fry rather than being simmered. When he sat down to eat the finished product, Blumenthal was impressed. It was attractive to look at and very tasty: its nut flavour and dry texture gave it individuality.

Another stop on the road was at the Osteria Francescana restaurant in Modena, run by maverick chef Massimo Bottura. There he noted the lengthy, attentive method that Bottura employed in order to make his pasta. Blumenthal admired both his unconventional air and his patient way in the kitchen. He also appreciated the chef's wistful, nostalgic attitude to cooking. As for the Bolognese he produced for Blumenthal, it was delicious and inspiring. Unlike at some other stops on the journey, garlic was used here, to Blumenthal's satisfaction. The sauce was rich, the pasta 'silky'. Again, it was an experience which Blumenthal found enjoyable and informative.

So it was that they drove south to Rome, to visit the home of La Pasta di Aldo, made by Luigi Donnari. He gave Blumenthal the benefit of his expert tuition on how to make great pasta and then invited his visitor to lunch with him and his family. It proved to be an elaborate affair, from the antipasta of stuffed olive and prosciutto through to the lemon and parsley-infused homemade pasta. Blumenthal was energised by his visit to Donnari whose fearsome devotion to his craft was, he felt, what perfection was all about.

The meal he enjoyed there was in sharp contrast to the dinner he and his crew had at their modest hotel later that evening, which he described as a typical venue for the outskirts of an airport. For now, though, it was time to fly home to Bray to put what he had learned into action.

To this end, he asked customers at The Hinds Head to blind-taste three separate samples of spaghetti Bolognese. The first two were the recipe he had devised as a result of his Italian trip, with different kinds of meat. The third was an everyday supermarket-style effort, with sauce from a jar and cheap, smelly Parmesan sauce. To his enormous relief, they chose the new recipe, with the smoother meat forming the more popular version of those two dishes. It was an enjoyable experiment for him: he got interesting answers and was able to interact with his customers. The end recipe that he presented to the world was one of the less challenging of the series. He advised his audience to increase the heat at the end of the preparation of the sauce in order to replicate the flavour of the sauce he had sampled at the Antica Trattoria.

Now it was time to seek the perfect bangers and mash, and, for this episode of the BBC series, he travelled closer to home – to Ludlow in Shropshire. It was a very Blumenthal-esque area. From its annual Food and Drink Festival to its Michelin-starred restaurants such as Hibiscus to the long queues at the local butcher's, it seemed a place that threatened to equal his passion for fine food. Heston often bemoans the comparative lack of passion that Brits seem to display for food compared with their continental equivalents, but, in Ludlow, he was able to taste a hint of culinary passion in the air and he was pleased with what he discovered on his visit. He enjoyed tasting the numerous varieties of sausages, although he was not seeking an actual sausage to include in his perfect dish. Rather he was aiming to understand what factors created the perfect banger so he could create his own masterpiece. In the course of his 'Banger Idol' quest, he discovered that Ludlow held a similar competition as part of its annual Festival, where five sausages would vie for the title of people's choice. During his trip, he was able to learn more about what made a good sausage. Most significantly, he concluded that filler was an important component. He must have tried scores of sausages because his shortlist for tasting back in Bray was 40-strong.

He and his colleagues cooked the sausages in the water bath and eagerly tried slices of each. Eventually, 40 became 10 as a shortlist was agreed upon. They were learning ever more specifically what made a sausage great: the correct texture, the seasoning, the meat and how it is packed, the optimum level of salting. The sausage that they felt best answered all of these requirements was a banger made by a company called Porkinson.

He then visited a Northumberland farm run by a passionate porkophile called Graham Head. He told Blumenthal that Middle White is the best breed of pig for sausage meat and passed on a wealth of wisdom, including everything from the importance of diet for the final two months of a pig's life to the flavour of the resultant pork. Before heading for home,

Blumenthal allowed the pig expert to cook him a bacon sandwich. Well, you would, wouldn't you?

Later, a Scottish butcher taught Blumenthal how to physically make the sausages.

His banger investigation over, it was time to turn to the mash. He already had potato expertise under his belt from the roast chicken and roast potato episode when he had visited the MBM base in Norfolk. There he had picked up a locker-room of anorak information, including the best temperature for storing potatoes destined for mashing (3 degrees Celsius, fact-fans). He lined up a shortlist of eight types of spuds and along with his colleagues in Bray tested them for mash potential. The winner was the Yukon Gold, which blew him and his colleagues away with its fluffy matter and tasty flavour. He thought it provided 'gutsy comfort food'.

The episode drew praise from reviewers. Brad Newsome wrote in *The Age*, 'Blumenthal is a natural and charismatic host, and the whole production is slickly put together.'

The Australian was also impressed: 'In his eight-part series, the stocky, oddly-groovy Blumenthal, his cool obsessiveness totally captivating, focuses on some of Britain's classic dishes, from fish and chips to roast beef. This week, bangers and mash and treacle tart get the Blumenthal treatment. Dressed in white coat and safety goggles, he scientifically dismantles the traditional recipes with liquid nitrogen and thermally-kinetic dry ice.'

In writing up his bangers and mash quest in the book that accompanied his series, Blumenthal advised people cooking sausages to 'go the whole hog', demonstrating his liking for puns. For example, when he is busy, he is happy to report that he 'has a lot on his plate' and, when writing of how phosphates hampered his progress with a particular dish, he concluded that 'phate was against us'. Later, when investigating the steak, he found that the porterhouse cut was hard to get in the UK, so 'portered it out' of his hunt. But it was in his fish and chips episode that he really went pun-crazy. He arrived at one venue and he said, 'This must be the plaice.' Having learned plenty there, he told his host he would take what he had been told and 'mullet over'. He visited an American-based fish and chip shop and marvelled at the puns on their noticeboard, which included 'The frequent fryers' club' and the jar that solicited 'fish'n'tips'.

It is to the steak episode of *In Search of Perfection* that we now turn. For this show he paid the first visit of his life to the place that never sleeps, New York City. There, he showed yet more boyishness and also confirmed that food is not the only subject of which he holds an anorak's knowledge. When he stood at the observation level high up on the famous Empire State Building, he looked out on to the blocks of Manhattan and observed the cinematic heritage of the city. Blumenthal spotted filming locations for movies including *King Kong*, *Superman*, *Hannah and Her Sisters*, *Kramer vs Kramer* and *North by Northwest*. It was not, at this point, a culinary survey of the city, but a cinematic one. He was also intoxicated by the lively, ambitious atmosphere of Manhattan. It was to prove a memorable and enjoyable visit for him.

His first step on the steak search was at Peter Luger in Brooklyn. Founded in 1887, it is a genuine institution that has won countless honours for its steaks over and over. Blumenthal's movie-world obsession was piqued the moment he walked into the place. With its manly atmosphere and table of suited men speaking Italian, he felt as though he had walked straight into an American gangster movie. He then met with Jody Storch, who had inherited the restaurant via a family legacy that stretched back generations. Not for the first time, Blumenthal found himself mourning the fact that Britain did not offer such a great focus on family food. Storch told him how she had studied from her childhood how to spot the best meat for steak. She showed him to the giant room where the steaks were 'aged' in a dry environment, the size of which surprised Blumenthal. In the city of skyscrapers, it seemed that even the storage rooms were enormous. He learned much from his time with Storch, but also realised that some questions were not going to be answered. All food experts liked to keep some of their secrets secret.

On day two of his trip, he put the steak search to one side and instead did a tour of the city's more famed eateries. He kicked off at The Empire Diner where he sampled an enormous breakfast. He was cheered by the huge quantities of food on the go and also noted another cinematic tie-in, recognising the venue from the opening titles of Woody Allen's *Manhattan*. His lunch was at the famous Lower East Side deli Katz's, which featured in a famous scene of another film, *When Harry Met Sally*. There Blumenthal tucked into

Katz's signature hot pastrami sandwich. In a city rich with venues offering such a sandwich – Carnegie Deli is perhaps the most celebrated – Katz's is nevertheless one of the leaders. Blumenthal enjoyed his lunch, rating the sandwich as one of the best he had ever eaten. He once more found himself ruefully contrasting the way the meat was prepared and served at Katz's with how things are often performed back in Britain. There was just time to sample a hot dog at Gray's – where he loved the food and the fun – before it was time to visit WD-50, a restaurant back in the Lower East Side. There, he bumped into his great rival Ferran Adrià of El Bulli. It's a small (culinary) world.

Having eaten so well, he also slept well.

On day three, he visited a strip joint. No, Blumenthal was not experiencing some sort of personal crisis; instead, he was visiting the famed Robert's Steakhouse, which just happens to be located in a gentleman's club. Having been given yet more education in the venue's kitchen, he sat down to be offered a sample of steaks which had been matured for different lengths of time. As he tucked into the meat, he attempted to not be too distracted by the dancing ladies of the venue. He was no stranger to fine meat but admitted that he was learning much from the experience. He and the head chef Adam Perry Lang spoke for hours, sharing their passion and knowledge. He might have been in New York rather than Bray, but Blumenthal felt perfectly at home.

There was an explosive incident one evening in New York while Blumenthal and his crew were relaxing over some drinks in Manhattan's The Spotted Pig with the restaurant's large, red-bearded, wild co-owner, Mario Batali. 'Mario produced this bottle of something strong and he was talking about how the English can't hold their drink,' recalled Blumenthal in a subsequent interview. 'Two hours later, he was slumped beside me with a cigarette in his mouth and his head swaying to loud music. I made a comment about what a nice room we were in and then he went to grab my nuts. So I grabbed his hand, then he pulled my hand up to his mouth, put one of my fingers into his mouth and started biting it.'

Blumenthal had to act fast. 'I thought, If I don't do something, he's going to bite my finger off,' he recalled. There was no time to waste. 'I jumped up, got behind him, stuck my free fingers in his nostrils and yanked his head back. Then I got carried away. I jumped on to the sofa and back-dived him so that my back hit his front.' The fight was over. 'Mario got up and went home,' said Blumenthal.

Once he was back at his real home, it was time for him and his colleagues to once more hit the development kitchen and taste some fine beef. They tried the Orkney, South Devon, Aberdeen Angus, Hereford and Red Poll. Blumenthal was less than blown away by these and was somewhat nervous as they turned to the final one to be tested – the Longhorn. Fortunately, this one gave him plenty to smile about. It was the obvious winner. He suggested that viewers serve it alongside blue-cheese-infused, butter pickled mushrooms, mushroom ketchup and a simple salad, including lettuce, tomatoes and dressing. Perfection, he believed.

While in New York, Blumenthal had done a bit of

research for another of his series dishes: fish and chips. But his investigation had begun in a backstreet of Lambeth in London at 6am. He was there to visit James Knight of Mayfair, a renowned fishmonger. Having talked over the options for the perfect fish for the traditional favourite, he left with six different types to put to the development-kitchen test: turbot, John Dory, Dover sole, brill, cod and plaice. He learned plenty about each fish type, including where they most liked to swim. Back in Bray, he and his team put each to the test and turbot emerged as the favourite, even after a supplementary test had been performed to ensure it hadn't just been a fluke.

He then referred back to what he had learned at the MBM centre about potatoes as he turned to the subject of the chips. While developing his triple-cooked chips for The Fat Duck, Blumenthal had undergone an investigation and level of experimentation that was extraordinary even by his standards. That dish had been first developed in 1993, so he had over a decade of form with his chips to draw on. Nonetheless, he was determined not to rest on his laurels, and set up a chip test in the kitchen. Having learned what temperature the chip-destined potatoes should be stored at (7 to 9 degrees Celsius) he was ready to test. Arran Victory was deemed the winner, beating even the Maris Piper which was his favoured potato for chips at The Hinds Head. The Arran Victory gave him what he wanted: the combination of a 'glass-like' exterior and a soft, fluffy inside.

The New York leg of his fish and chip search came at a Manhattan chippie called A Salt & Battery. Blumenthal adored the place, at which he ticked off a mental list of authentic British chippie features, all bound together into one glorious Greenwich Village venue. He loved it all, including the cans of one of his favourite drinks, Dandelion & Burdock. Outside, he noted the Union Jack-painted red Mini Cooper, belonging to the owner, who came from Accrington and was the son of a chippie-owning couple.

Clearly, as we have seen, Blumenthal is a man who can be transported back in time by food. For him, eating is like a time machine. Fish and chips are an evocative dish for even the least imaginative of minds, so for a brain as thoughtful as Blumenthal's it is a rich mine of memories. To this end, he encouraged viewers to take the nostalgia one step further. He told them to purchase a jar of pickled onions – the traditional accompaniment to fish and chip shops in Britain – and an atomiser spray. The pickling juice from the jar should be poured into the atomiser and sprayed either over the chips themselves or round the room that they would be eaten in. The diner can then tuck in and enjoy the memories.

This episode caught the attention of the prestigious *New York Times*, where Harold McGee wrote, 'A more reliable innovation comes from Heston Blumenthal, chef at The Fat Duck near London. Mr Blumenthal recently undertook a series for BBC 2 television and a book, both called *In Search of Perfection*, in which he updated classic British foods. His beer batter for fish and chips, developed with The Fat Duck's research manager, Christopher Young, is unusual in two ways. It's squirted as a foam from a soda siphon – the sure sign of a post-Ferran Adrià preparation – and half of its liquid is vodka. The siphon makes things easier if you have more than a few batches to fry, but even without a siphon the vodka is an excellent trick.'

The show was also written up in the South African evening newspaper *Tonight*. 'He takes the meal to extraordinary lengths,' wrote Bianca Coleman. 'The chips are prepared in several stages – par-boiling, drying in the fridge, the first frying, again in the fridge and the final frying. All this after selecting the right kind of potato. The batter includes vodka, beer and a carbonated bottle. I giggled at the pretentiousness of Blumenthal's squirt of "onion juice" – the vinegar from a jar of pickled onions.'

The next dish on the perfection menu was Black Forest Gateau. This was another foodstuff that Blumenthal had a bit of history with – and not entirely happily. Those visits to Berni Inns had all too often ended with a Black Forest Gateau arriving at the table. He was almost always bitterly disappointed by the cake; even when he tried to scoop the chocolate off to eat alone; he would feel let down. Moreover, the cake had become something of a laughing stock in Britain. Or, perhaps more accurately, a sneering stock. This fact, though, was one of the reasons he chose it: he found the attitudes to the dish were sometimes so snotty that he felt almost protective of it. This was part of a wider Blumenthal philosophy: no food deserves to be sneered at because, if it is produced correctly, it cannot be wrong. Fired up, he set out to research the perfect Black Forest Gateau.

His journey began in the somewhat surprising surroundings of Pisa in Italy. It had made sense for him to visit Italy in his spaghetti Bolognese quest, but to journey there on this later quest was an eyebrow raiser. The reason for his choice was that, following a thorough testing of a number of chocolates for the gateau, he and his team had agreed that Amedei Chuao was the most suitable. He was full of enthusiasm for the chocolate, so much so that he nearly declared that it 'captured the romance' of the Black Forest, which would have been an embarrassing thing to be seen saying on camera, because at this point he had never visited the region. In Pisa, he was shown around the Amedei operation, a complicated and spectacular affair that had Blumenthal's Willy Wonka side enraptured. He loved the smells – red berries, plum and leather among them – and the sounds of gloopy chocolate in production that echoed round the place. He sampled the product throughout the process, from a bitter liqueur right through to chocolate heaven. He shook his head in joyous disbelief at the final product, noting a tobacco element to the flavour. He joked that he felt like he was attending a wine-tasting session.

Next on his itinerary was the German town of Baden-Baden, an affluent area, which was to find infamy in the UK when the England national football team stayed there, allowing their wives and girlfriends ('WAGS') to soak up the wealthy air as they strolled from boutique to boutique, spending thousands of pounds on clothes and other essentials. There, he sampled the Schwarzwalder kirschtorte, which is the German origin of the Black Forest Gateau. Later, he was shown how to make the cake by cafe owner Volker Gmeiner. It was to prove an instructive conversation: when Blumenthal told Gmeiner how the British made the dish, his cheeky host responded, 'I get the impression they did everything wrong they could.' He then set about teaching his guest how to do everything right. By the end of the process, a perfect cake had been made, with Volker arguing that the holes and other imperfections were what made it perfect.

Having visited an alcohol distiller to learn about the perfect kirsch, Blumenthal was ready to put together his own perfect cake along with his pastry chef Jocky. He wanted to include the four tastes that Volker had told him were essential: sweet, sour, salt and bitter. They decided on six layers including a madeleine biscuit base, ganache and chocolate mousse. As ever, there was an eccentric final flourish from Blumenthal. He recommended filling an atomiser with kirsch and spraying it round the room before eating it. He also suggested serving the cake on a wooden base. Here, one commentator noted, Blumenthal captured the zeitgeist. Mark Palmer, writing in the *Daily Telegraph*, put his resurrection of the dish alongside a prawn cocktail revival. 'Even celebrity chef Heston Blumenthal saw fit to include Black Forest Gateau as one of his prized dishes on the recent BBC series *In Search of Perfection*, while the classic cookery book, *The Prawn Cocktail Years*, is back in print and selling like... like the Bay City Rollers used to in 1975,' he wrote.

Waltham Place Farm in the Berkshire village of White Waltham was a mere ten-minute drive away from

Blumenthal's base. Nonetheless, he had to make an early start because cow milking is an early-morning activity – and one that was new to Blumenthal. Guided by a farmer, who reminded Blumenthal more of a rocker with his huge moustache merging into a substantial pair of mutton chops, he was shown how to milk a cow. Blumenthal was surprised by how difficult it was when he got to work on the teats of his selected cow, Peggy. His hands began to tire and hurt before he had produced anything like the considerable quantity required. He let the farmer replace him at the teats and soon they had several litres of fresh milk. These would form the ice cream which would be served with his next perfection-quest dish: treacle tart.

Just as his farmer host had shown Blumenthal the cow-milking ropes, so did the chef introduce the farmer to a bit of his world. He had brought along a vat of his beloved liquid nitrogen, and he proceeded to produce ice cream using milk that had been obtained from Peggy the cow just 240 seconds earlier. That, he noted, was superfast work. His host was impressed with the final result, too. 'Mmm, that's rich, that is,' he said with a smile.

Rich too is the taste of Tate & Lyle treacle and it was to that company's headquarters in London's Docklands that Blumenthal now turned. Having been told of the biblical story that inspired the company's logo (how Samson killed a lion and bees made a honeycomb from its corpse), he was given another Willy Wonka-esque tour of a factory where he watched, listened and smelled everything as he was shown round.

Next, he visited the kitchens at Hampton Court. Like the Waltham Place Farm – from which The Fat Duck had been ordering produce for some time – this was a return to familiar territory. The workers here were historically minded, reproducing the exact hardware and ingredients of old to attempt to create authentic final products. It was a venture that was both ambitious and eccentric; no wonder Blumenthal felt at home. He was shown sugar from Iran and quotes from recipes from as far back as 1594, as he was given a history lesson in the origin of the tart. The attention to detail was immense: right down to using sugar with low water content to produce a historically accurate crust. His final step of the journey was in Berkshire, just as the first one had been. At Reading University, he was shown to a hi-tech smelling machine that gave him the chance to sample different flavours and smells that he could consider using in his perfect treacle tart.

Back in the Bray development kitchen, they tried numerous ingredients and methods as they pursued perfection in the form of a treacle tart. Once more, his water bath was used to cook a tin of golden syrup on a low heat for a number of weeks. He felt the wait was worth it, as the syrup took on extra depth. Finally, he had his line-up. Mindful of the hazards of liquid nitrogen in the wrong hands, not to mention the difficulty in obtaining it, he suggested his viewers use dry ice instead. It would still give the same dramatic misty effect, but would allow him and the BBC to sleep better at night, rather than fear headlines about liquid-nitrogen disasters.

The show had been enjoyable and successful, and the BBC happily commissioned a second series, entitled *Further Adventures in Search of Perfection*. Ahead of the second series, he explained what the basic parameters of his criteria were. 'We wanted the dishes to be ones that we are used to. Dishes we might not eat very often, but that have a certain nostalgia for most of us. And we also have to choose dishes that will have the audience thinking, I wonder how he's going to do that one?'

The first episode of *Further Adventures in Search of Perfection* saw Blumenthal return to New York. This time, his tireless quest was not for the perfect steak but for its fast-food relative, the hamburger. However, it was not in New York that his search began, but New Haven. There he headed straight to Louis' Lunch, a restaurant with a history (it opened back in 1895) and one that was dominated by the dish of the hour: the hamburger. There, Jeff Lassen showed Blumenthal how his venue put together a delicious hamburger. Salt levels, the patty, the bun and the right toppings were among the many subjects discussed, although Blumenthal's curiosity ran into a brick wall when he delved too deeply into the secrets of the place. When he asked what the exact recipe was, he was told, 'I'd have to put a gun to my head if I told you that.'

He watched Lassen cook the patties in an ancient grill that cooked both sides at once – there was none of your flipping going on here. The burgers at Louis' Lunch were served in toast, not buns, because that was how it had traditionally been done and Blumenthal noted that they used a toaster that was made in 1929. He approved. He also approved of the final product. 'Mmm,' he said on sampling the burger. 'This is really superb.' His quest for burger perfection was very much under way.

It was time for him to return at last to New York, where he was to visit the Shake Shack, a roadside food stand based in Madison Square Park. It produced hugely celebrated burgers, with publications as prestigious as *Time Out New York* and the *New York Times* both heartily recommending it to their readers. However, the vote of confidence that most struck Blumenthal came in the form of a lengthy queue of excited customers. There were at least 40 ahead of him when he arrived. He amused himself by reading the jokey placards that had been placed along the length of the queue to entertain customers.

Finally, he reached the front of the queue and placed his order. Some ten minutes later, he was handed his Shackburger and sat down to eat it while the camera crew filmed him. Even in cool New York, this proved something of a spectacle and he felt self-conscious as he combined the tricky task of eating a burger without making a mess of his clothes while describing to the camera what he was experiencing. One onlooker took photographs of him, which hardly increased his comfort levels. He then spoke to Shack man Richard Coraine about how he had put together the recipe for his perfect burger. He told Blumenthal his quest took him 'about six months, I racked up 10,000 miles and 30,000 calories!' Having discussed all the elements, Blumenthal again hit a brick wall of secrecy when he asked about the grinding of the meat and the sauce.

Next, he visited the Le Parker Meridien Hotel where an anonymous, furtive outlet – known by locals as Burger Joint – existed. It had proved hard to find the venue, not least because the producers declined to assist Blumenthal, hoping for some entertaining footage of him wandering around lost in New York. When he finally discovered the venue, he ordered a burger called The Works, which – as its name suggested – included everything from lettuce and tomato to pickle and mustard. He loved the resultant burger and was given plentiful details – including the mince grind size that the Shack had declined to share – about how it was made. He also noted with approval the way that the venue had been decorated with pictures of cultural icons. This context, he felt, added to the enjoyment of the food.

His final stop in America was at the workplace of an old friend. Thomas Keller runs several high-class restaurants in America and it was at the Bouchon Bakery that Blumenthal visited him to enquire about his Wagyu Beef Slider burger. This was a miniature burger in a brioche bun, which Blumenthal absolutely loved eating. His pal gave him the lowdown on its secrets and also explained that the dish had come about because he did not want to waste off-cuts from another dish.

Back home in the UK, Blumenthal had one more stop to make before taking what he had learned into the kitchen. Having visited a Knightsbridge butcher called Jack O'Shea and cooked samples of his meat on an impromptu pavement barbeque, he settled for chuck, brisket and short rib cuts to form the basis of the patty. For the bun, he followed a basic equation that human beings can generally open their jaws enough to put two or three fingers in. Such mathematics guided him to the perfect burger which he tutored his viewers on how to prepare and cook. It had been an enjoyable episode that indicated that much fun was on its way in series two.

Writing up the episode in the *Daily Mirror*, Jane Simon focused on his novel way with cheese when she said, 'When it comes to a barbie we all slap a processed cheese slice on our burgers. Maybe we might grate a bit of cheddar. But Heston, trying to create the perfect cheese slice, uses cystitis medicine. What on earth is breakfast like chez Blumenthal? I shudder to think how he makes Coco-Pops.'

The *Guardian*'s witty Charlie Brooker also commented on the burger edition. 'Each week, Heston, who really ought to buy a new pair of glasses because the ones he has are completely the wrong shape for his face and the lenses are so thick his eyes resemble a pair of olives hovering somewhere behind his head, possibly in another dimension and it all makes him look a bit like a mad German doctor performing experiments in a horror movie ... each week, Heston takes a classic dish (chicken tikka masala last week; hamburgers this week) and decides to create the "perfect" version of it. The end result looks suspiciously like a Burger King Whopper, albeit at 50 times the cost. It probably tastes 50 times better too but I'd be astonished if a single viewer follows the recipe to the letter. Building your own nuclear warhead would be simpler and once you'd made it you could terrorise millions into cooking you as many burgers as you wanted, home-made cheese slices and all. Still, it's fun to watch Mister Impossible doing his experiments. It's nice to know he's out there, even if you'll never taste the results. It's a pointless job, but somebody's got to do it.'

In the fish pie episode, Blumenthal reached new heights of eccentricity including sending an American student into a sound booth with plates of oyster and cooking fish over a barbeque using a squirrel trap in The Hinds Head car park. However, the search began at the break of day on a trawler just off Clyde. He was there to watch as some of the billion-strong population of langoustines were caught. He is a fan of the fish, particularly in fish pies, because their rich flavour helps counteract what he sees as the biggest potential drawback of the dish: its tendency to blandness. He was not just alongside fishermen but students, too, as Glasgow University was involved in a study of langoustines and Blumenthal found himself chatting with a professor as they watched the fish get caught. They discussed how the tail of the langoustine is the part that is most tasty, and noticed how the more red the fish were on catching, the more stressed they were, which contributed to an impairment of the flavour. This was attention to detail indeed – but, of course, the most important detail was what they tasted like and Blumenthal found the one he ate 'wonderfully sweet'.

In the next leg of his journey, he was shown eating a bowl of clam chowder in Connecticut, in a piece of footage that had been shot during his American hamburger quest. Then it was back to The Hinds Head car park in Bray, for a most entertaining scene. He cooked a pair of cured haddock fillets in a hay-stuffed squirrel cage trap over a barbeque. You don't get that sort of activity on *Ready Steady Cook*. The hay element had history, having long been used to cook ham, and Blumenthal had employed it for several Fat Duck dishes including triple-cooked chips. He hoped that it would lend a subtle smoke flavour to the haddock and only lightly cook the fish, which had yet to be placed into the pie proper for further cooking. He was delighted with the speed of the squirrel-cage operation (just 60 seconds) and with the result.

It was time for him to return to Oxford University, the scene of the crisps-eating test with the microphone and amplifier, under the watchful eye of Professor Charles Spence. This time he sent a Californian student called Carmel into the booth with some oysters to eat. Some she ate to a soundtrack of farm sounds, the others to a soundtrack of the sound of the sea. She found the latter oysters far more authentic. He recommended that, to accompany the final dish, viewers should listen to the sounds of the sea, and a suitable tune was placed on the BBC website for viewers to download. He even included 'sand' in the recipe, in the shape of panko and shirasu, and foaming seawater sauce made from shallot, garlic, vermouth and white wine.

His search for the perfect risotto began at Carlo Cracco's Milan restaurant, an artful establishment that used carnaroli rice in an extravagant risotto dish. Here, the chef showed Blumenthal how they prepared their dish using fresh rice, but assured him that non-fresh rice would not be out of the question for a tasty final product. The two soon found common ground and were happily discussing yet more adventurous possibilities in the preparation of risotto. Blumenthal suggested cooking fresh rice, then using the same water to cook non-fresh rice. Cracco roared with laughter and approval at the suggestion. For the Italian was no stranger to invention himself, as he proved when he served Blumenthal a second risotto, flavoured with sea urchins and instant coffee. For an Italian even to own instant coffee was surprising, and that he would use it in the preparation of risotto was stunning.

Then it was time for him to pay a first-hand visit to a Fat Duck supplier – the Rondolino family's rice fields in Piedmont. He was enthralled by the rice fields, describing them as resembling 'vast sheets of glass' which were viewable for many miles. There he was given more information than anyone could ever want about the mechanics and minutiae of rice. He and his host competed to come up with the most geeky rice detail, with phrases such as 'lipids in the rice' and 'surface proteins oxidising' filled the air. Speaking of which, he had always enjoyed the nutlike taste of the rice made by the Rondolinos and was pleased to smell it in the air when he visited their fields. He was then given a magnifying glass through which he viewed individual grains of rice.

Gualtiero Marchesi – the first Italian to win three

Michelin stars – invited Blumenthal to his Milan restaurant. There, he served his guest an exquisite risotto, finished off with gold leaf, of all things. However, equally of interest to Blumenthal was the posh art that was dotted around the venue. He wondered how much of an effect these visuals had on the eating experience. In Bray, he conducted a clever experiment to test the relationship between food and visual environment. He asked a man called Alberto to test three differently named risottos and say which he liked most. However, the truth was that the only substantial difference between the three was their name and the fact that one had strawberries served with it. This proved to Blumenthal that the presentation and name of a dish made a major difference to how a person enjoyed it.

His Peking-duck episode began where so many others had ended: in his kitchen in Bray. There, he tasted three separate domestic crispy-duck dishes to get a measure of the good, the bad and the ugly of the dish before jetting off to Beijing to research further. He checked in at the Crown Plaza Beijing and strolled around the breathtaking Wangfujing street market, where he was confronted by a cacophony of noise, colours and smells. In the modern corporate stores such as Nike and Armani, such Western commercials as a huge poster of David Beckham were unmissable sights. However, watching the workers tout everything from squid on stick to cockroaches, scorpions and seahorses was far more appealing to Blumenthal. He also noted stalls selling silkworm and centipede. He sniffed simmering tripe, and described the smell as 'faecal'. He wisely left that where it was but tucked into first some eel and then some dumpling soup.

The following day, he met a Chinese chef called Da Dong. He found his visit to Dong's restaurant akin to being 'on the stage of an opera', so vast and detailed was the establishment. When he was shown the Chinese way of removing the duck's insides, he found time to squeeze in another poor pun: 'It's like a new martial art,' he told Dong, 'tae kwak do.'

He was informed that they used fruit-tree wood for the cooking, which maintained a consistent temperature and imposed an agreeable fragrance on the duck.

Closer to home, Georgina Campbell, in the *Independent*, reported on one of the pit-stops Blumenthal made in his journey. 'Imagine yourself going quietly about your business on your farm in Emyvale, Co Monaghan, when a phone call comes in from Heston Blumenthal's experimental kitchen in Bray, Berkshire (called, appropriately enough, The Fat Duck), just wondering if a couple of the team could pop over for a look some day,' she began. 'It may have sounded like a hoax to the staff at Silver Hill Foods at first. Lyla Steele chuckles as she recalls the visit: "We were in shock, and still are, but they were great crack."'

Blumenthal tended to make friends, and sometimes influence people, wherever he stopped and the duck farm was no exception.

For the chicken tikka masala episode, Blumenthal flew all the way to – where else? – India. Curry forms the second half of Blumenthal's domestic culinary rulebook. As we have seen, he makes sure that he has a family meal on Sunday evening, in the shape of a traditional Sunday dinner and on Monday evening it is always a curry for him. He also visits Pizza Express restaurants and the local kebab van in Marlow. Sometimes he ventures to one of his favourite London restaurants including Rasoi, Zaika and Benares. Oftentimes, however, he grabs a takeaway from his award-winning local in Cookham – Malik's. That restaurant would form part of his journey in search of the perfect chicken tikka masala. First, though, it was time for him to wave goodbye to his wife and children and take a plane to India.

Just as he'd arrived in China at night, he landed in Delhi in the early hours of the morning and was aghast at how hot and hectic the city was at such an hour. It was to be a taxing visit for him. After resting, he visited the Moti Mahal restaurant near Netaji Subhash Marg. This was a venue that was the spiritual home of the chicken tikka masala dish and Blumenthal was shown round by proprietor Vinod Chadha, who made him feel very welcome in the stiflingly hot kitchen. All the same, he was a frustrating man to interview on television, partly due to translation issues, partly because he consistently addressed his remarks to the crew's director rather than Blumenthal. Yet Chadha was informative, showing how the chicken meat is made tender and flavoured, a lengthy and loving process and one he outlined with charm and passion. It was soon time for the marinated chicken to be cooked in the huge tandoor oven which the venue had been using since 1947. Chadha theatrically presented Blumenthal with a sample of the finished product.

It impressed him, and he felt it was a nicely balanced product all round.

The spice market in Old Delhi is a place that Blumenthal will not forget in a hurry. The moment he arrived in its alleys, the ever-observant superchef was intoxicated by the colours, noise and scents. However, when he reached the area where huge sacks of chilli were kept, the effect became almost overwhelming and Blumenthal was soon almost choking. He noticed that his camera crew, too, were coughing uncontrollably. However, this was not just something affecting visitors. The locals, too, were struggling with the chilli-infused air as a soundtrack of coughing and throat-clearing filled the air.

Back in Britain, he visited the Magnetic Resonance Research Centre in Cambridge where he made a typically eccentric request: he asked the scientists to run an MRI scan – in which a magnetic field and radio waves are used to create computer images of tissues, organs and other structures inside a body – over three chicken breasts, each with a different marinade. He felt this was the best way to find out whether – and if so how deeply – a marinade penetrated a piece of meat. Although a little amused by the suggestion, the scientists soon became enthusiastic as the results showed how important yoghurt and ginger were to the mix and also confirmed that overnight marinating did have an effect. 'There is a whole family of other tests you could do,' said one, 'to explore structural questions, such as texture and tenderness of the marinated chicken or how the marinade travels along the fibres.' Now they were talking Blumenthal's language.

After a visit to his local Indian restaurant and a good chat with owner Malik that left him even more educated about the ins and outs of chicken tikka masala, Blumenthal felt suitably empowered to produce his own perfect take on the dish. He decided that the first essential to this end was for him to have his own tandoor oven. This was built in the corner of the car park of The Hinds Head. First, he asked two of his colleagues to hand-dig the required hole. A director suggested that the soundtrack of the *Reservoir Dogs* movie be played over the footage to provide dramatic atmosphere. However, within minutes of starting, they gave up after their shovels began to hit rock in the ground.

A professional digger was sent for and the ever-curious Blumenthal watched as the professional team dug lower and lower into the ground. His inner child prompted him to have a go on the machine which reminded him of the sort of thing one might see on the kids' classic *Thunderbirds*. He took a while to master how it worked but was soon making a reasonable job of it. He could not resist making a mock surge towards his colleagues, just long enough for them to fear that he was about to run them over. Happy days. The tandoor was built and the final brick was put in place by Blumenthal himself in a ceremonial moment. It reached temperatures of 500 degrees Celsius, to his considerable delight.

Caitlin Moran of *The Times* was impressed. 'Blumenthal is a striking maverick in the world of TV chefs,' she said. 'For starters, while all the rest are sexy chicks and honest geezers, Blumenthal – in his white lab coat, rubber gloves, square glasses and shaved head – looks greatly like Les from *Vic Reeves Big Night Out*, although, presumably, he isn't scared of chives. And while all the rest are about "bish-bash-bosh", "quick, easy and delicious" and keeping food "simple" and "real", Blumenthal is happy to spend all day placing cardamom pods into a vacuum, putting turnips in particle accelerators, and launching brie into space. The difference between the "money shots" – bits where they actually eat the food – for him and Nigella Lawson are comically vast. Nigella will climb into bed with a bread and butter pudding, smear it all over her luscious embonpoint, and scream "I'M COMING!" as she spoons the lot down with wolverine vigour. Blumenthal, on the other hand – after a solid half-hour devoted to making a single bowl of curry – eats a spoonful and then pauses, looking like the Terminator assessing fresh data with his mouth. "Now that is my perfect chicken tikka masala," he says, very simply, as a statement of total curry fact.'

It was time to turn up the temperature a bit... from masala to chilli con carne. The International Chilli Society is a non-profit organisation that arranges 'chilli cook-offs'. 'Our sole purpose is to promote, develop and improve the preparation and appreciation of true chilli,' runs its mission statement. It is a noble enough aim and Blumenthal attended one of the group's famous events in Washington DC, where he found a loud, crowded affair populated by all manner of people from wholesome American lads to Goths, men in kilts and 'chilli queens'. It was a raucous atmosphere: loud skinheads stood necking cartons of chilli con carne as if they were glasses of whisky. Teams competed in this chilli cook-off not just with the food they produced, but also with increasingly attention-grabbing names. Just a selection of those that took Blumenthal's attention included Rage Against the Cuisine and Eternal Chilli of Life. Another grabbed his attention not so much for its name, but for the slogan that accompanied it: 'Jack's Chili – If you haven't eaten Jack's Chili, you don't know Jack.' He was reminded of the American cartoon *The Simpsons*.

He asked around, got the lowdown on who was expected to win and made a beeline for their stalls. First up, he visited a man called Dan Bauer, whose chilli con carne name was Cowboy Chilli Too. The cowboy hat-wearing Bauer talked through his tips for a perfect chilli. He was initially forthcoming, mentioning for instance that he believed in using dry chillies rather than fresh ones. However, as Blumenthal pressed him for more and more details, he said he would not reveal the final thing that he spooned into his recipe. Others, though, did give him their secrets, and Blumenthal noted that chocolate regularly recurred. He found one contestant who used white hominy beans and another who added a touch of cumin to the mix. In the end, it was Bauer's wife Janie who won the cook-off, though Blumenthal hadn't spoken with her.

Back at the testing kitchen, his colleagues lined up 11 bowls, each with a different chilli powder. He had the distinct impression that at least one of them was going to be painfully hot. His money was on the bowls that were labelled Somalian Extra Hot and, indeed, Devil's Penis, a name to strike fear into any man. The genitally named powder did indeed turn out to be a fiery affair. Quite literally: he imagined fire as he ate it and sweat poured from his face. He tried to speak to the camera about what he was experiencing but could hardly get his words out. The Somalian Extra Hot also lived up to its name, but even the seemingly innocuous Birds' Eye chilli shook him with its potency. He felt as though someone had stuck a Bunsen burner in his mouth and lit the gas. Something that even in the oddball atmosphere of The Fat Duck development kitchen would be a bit much to cope with.

Next came the episode's most eccentric moment, as Blumenthal and the crew drove to Nottingham University School of Physics to use their MRI scanner. He wanted to examine the effect that eating chilli had on the brain, and what better way than to be scanned as one ate it? Because of the metal plate that had been put into his back after his childhood accident, Blumenthal could not go into the scanner himself. So he took along his head chef Ashley Watts as the guinea pig, to spend 45 minutes in the cramped scanner having chilli fed to him. The session came to an end when some chilli oil accidentally went into Watts's eye rather than his mouth. Enough was enough – but Blumenthal had scientifically confirmed that eating hot food such as chilli activated emotional parts of the brain.

He later returned to Oxford University to use its gas chromatograph, which he had first used in the treacle tart episode. This was one element of the episode that got the critics talking. James Walton wrote in the *Daily Telegraph*:

'Of course it's the mad science we're after and last night's episode certainly didn't let us down. The man was on fairly laddish form himself. He and his chef mates also went for plenty of blokey joshing about who could take the hottest food. Discovering, for example, that American chilli con carne often contains bourbon, Blumenthal attached a bottle of Jack Daniel's to a gas chromatograph. He then identified as many of its separate smells as possible to establish which of them adds to the flavour (although not why this matters).'

Next, in exploring the trifle, Blumenthal was on suitable ground for a perfection quest. After all, it was Michelangelo who said, 'Trifles make perfection and perfection is no trifle.' One man who would agree is the owner of Low Sizergh, an organic farm in the heart of the Lake District. He assembled what he described as a 'shrine to trifle' for Blumenthal. Here was the man to speak to about the dish. He presented Blumenthal with everything from a representation of the 1660 original trifle recipe to a more evolved version which included sprinkles of bread. Blumenthal enjoyed sampling the ever-evolving versions of the trifle that his Cumbrian host presented him with and offered positive feedback. 'Texturally interesting' was his verdict on one of them. He later identified a 'fleeting, mercurial and elusive' taste of cinnamon. By this time, they had arrived at 1751 in the history of the trifle, in the comprehensive history lesson that Low Sizergh's owner was giving Blumenthal, a willing, enthusiastic pupil to the end. When they ate the 1751 version, he warned his host that he 'might need to make some more'. Blumenthal added that he found it 'absolutely delicious. Trifle's usually thought of as something cheap and nasty. A bowl of gloop. But this has a range of distinct flavours and textures – a real complexity. There's a great sense of contrasts in the experience of eating it.'

He was a huge step closer to trifle perfection and his lesson at the shrine to the dish was over. As they regarded the aftermath of the lesson, the Low Sizergh boss turned to Blumenthal and said, 'It has been a Mad Hatter's tea party.' *Alice in Wonderland* fan Blumenthal thoroughly approved.

Next up, he took a flight to the Netherlands. The Centre For Food Sciences at Wageningen University is a very Blumenthal-esque place. His host Jon Prinz was – according to the visiting chef – 'brilliant and barking mad in equal measure'. He should know – he had worked with Prinz before on an experiment where he made Blumenthal put headphones on so he could hear the crunching noise he was making while he chewed gum. Just the sort of scientific food japes that Blumenthal enjoys; no wonder he returned for more. This time, it was a custard-testing venture that Prinz had lined up for his visitor. One part of the test involved Blumenthal eating a custard that had been laced with sand to make it more crunchy. Not exactly conventional cooking, but as nothing compared to what came next. To show how much food residue remains in the mouth after swallowing, Prinz invited Blumenthal to place a tampon in his mouth after swallowing a mouthful of custard. With the tampon's string hanging out of his mouth, Blumenthal looked quite a sight, but he was ready to return home and put together what he hoped would be a perfect trifle. This was a dish that spawned variants in The Fat Duck menu, including a strawberry and olive oil combination.

Further Adventures in Search of Perfection had been a roaring success and had made Blumenthal more recognisable. The fame he acquired from these television appearances soon led to his being invited to the studios of BBC Radio to take part in one of the most prestigious shows in the history of the corporation: *Desert Island Discs*. First broadcast in 1942, the show has become a national institution. Guests are invited to select which eight records they would take with them to a desert island. They also name one book and one luxury. According to the *Guinness Book of Records*, it is the longest-running music show in radio history. Here was confirmation of Blumenthal's stature.

His choices gave an interesting insight into the man. His first choice was 'Ana Fil Houb' by Lil Boniche, a Sephardic Jewish composer of Andalusian-Arab music. So far so obscure, but Blumenthal's next selection was better known: 'Man with a Harmonica' from the soundtrack of *Once Upon a Time in the West* by Ennio Morricone, the award-winning composer of numerous movie scores including those for *The Good, The Bad and The Ugly*, *A Fistful Of Dollars* and *Once Upon a Time in America*. 'Man with a Harmonica' is a slowly building tune that oozes the spirit of the Western movie, with a screeching and haunting harmonica.

Then came a more up-tempo choice: the funky 'Every

Dub' by The Sunburst Band, followed by a Bobby Womack tune. Womack is musical royalty, having been inducted into the Rock And Roll Hall of Fame in April 2009. His material has straddled many musical genres and his 'Love Has Finally Come at Last' is a funk-fused easy listening classic. Next up was a flamenco song, 'Entre Dos Aguas' by Paco de Lucia, first released in 1973. From flamenco guitars to 'Harry the Guitar' – the next song choice was by Dr Rubberfunk, the jazz/funk artist. This was not proving to be a list full of commercial crowd-pleasers, but then Blumenthal's cooking has never been mass-market either. Ilham Al Madfai is an Iraqi composer who was once so popular that he was known as the Baghdad Beatle. An accomplished guitarist, he has produced many catchy songs, not least 'Chal Chal Alayea el Rumman', Blumenthal's choice on the show. His final selection was Verdi's 'The Grand March' performed by Orchestra e Coro del Teatro alla Scala.

After his musical selections, the conversation turned to Blumenthal's choice of book and luxury – both were food related. The book he would take to a desert island was *On Food and Cooking* by Harold McGee and the luxury would be Japanese knives.

His appearance provoked comment. 'Blumenthal made for a delightful guest,' wrote Laura Barton on her *Guardian* blog. 'He appears to have a genuine sense of curiosity and he told lovely stories about staying up until 2am experimenting with creme brulee; translating French cookery books word-for-word; his earlier life as a debt collector and the day he sent his wife to the supermarket to see which potatoes had the greatest density (the denser the potato the better the chips, apparently). Although Blumenthal is evidently eager to explore new musical flavours, there was undoubtedly a prevailing sense of dinner party music.'

Meanwhile, work continued as normal for Blumenthal back at The Fat Duck. In 2007, he completed work on one of the most ambitious and famous of Fat Duck dishes: Sound of the Sea. He had a long-held ambition to have what he called a 'sound course' on the restaurant's menu after playing around with ideas in the Oxford laboratory of a man called Charles Spence. He would wear headphones that increased the natural sounds of chewing food. He played around with different ideas and found that merely altering the sound heard through the headphones could make it seem that the food he was eating was more crisp or crunchy. The food had not changed, but altering the sound made it seem like it had. In Spencer, Blumenthal had found a true ally. Both were boundless enthusiasts and had a healthy streak of eccentricity to supplement their energy. Between them, they were bound to stumble across some great ideas and have plenty of fun as they did so.

They fed a group of people some oysters, but half of the people ate with a background track of ocean-related sounds, the other half ate with the sounds of a farmyard. It was not a shock that those who ate to the sound of the ocean found that the oysters tasted saltier, but it piqued Blumenthal and Spencer's curiosity further. They tried a similar test on a larger group of people. This time, those being tested were fed egg and bacon ice cream, once to a backdrop of a sizzling bacon sound, then to a soundtrack of clucking chickens. The audience reported that, sure enough, the sound of chickens made the ice cream taste more egg-like. It had been identical food for both sittings, but the sound had significantly altered the taste experience of those eating. Blumenthal and his colleague were delighted with the result.

Blumenthal was keen to introduce this knowledge to a Fat Duck dish. When he was feeling bold – and when the restaurant was suitably quiet – he invited regular customers to wear headphones and discover the effect that an increase in the volume of their crunching of the food would have on the experience. He then slowly introduced a sound course, which he invited customers to take part in by way of a card given to them during a previous course. He did not want to make the sound course compulsory, so customers would opt to take part by ticking a box on the card. After much fevered experimentation, he introduced the sound by way of an iPod placed inside a large conch shell. The sounds of the sea are then relayed to the diner from many angles, transporting them to the seaside as they eat the dish that includes oysters, clams and sea urchins. Tapioca flour was included to represent sand and seaweed was also on the menu. There was also a foam effect to the 'sea' element of the food, including leek, cockles and white wine.

Along the way of the development of this spectacular, ambitious course, there had been numerous ideas tossed around by Blumenthal and his staff. There was talk of the waiter wearing aqua-diving gear to serve the food. Another suggestion was that there should be a tray of sand placed under the table, so the customers could be standing in sand as they ate. The chef himself briefly considered including a glass of 'sea-flavoured' water with the food. However, as he writes in *The Big Fat Duck Cookbook*, 'part of the art of creating a dish is knowing where to draw the line'. With the line drawn, he completed the dish in 2007 and began serving it to customers who had ticked the box on the card. Naturally, this imaginative dish captured the imagination of the public and the media who lapped up the details. Blumenthal became 'that guy who uses iPods as part of his food'.

So 2007 had proven to be a particularly experimental year for Blumenthal. For some time, he had been interested in creating a dish that represented the gifts of the biblical three wise men: gold, frankincense and myrrh. The fact that a Christmas special of ...*Perfection* had been commissioned gave him the, well, perfect time to bring the idea to fruition.

He travelled to Oman and researched the origins and usages of all three ingredients. Back in England, the dish kicked off with a communion wafer that had been given the scent of a freshly bathed baby. This was followed by an ingenious combination of a golden ingot with a teapot full of frankincense water stirred using a branch of myrrh. The resulting liquid was poured over a plate including a gel, royale and roulade. The end result became a dish on the a la carte menu at The Fat Duck. Just as he had looked east for inspiration for this dish, so too did he for the ballotine of Anjou pigeon that was added to the tasting menu in the same year. He included what appeared to be a prawn cracker, but one that was actually flavoured with pigeon and duck.

A 2007 addition to the a la carte menu was a beef royal. Its introduction is of interest primarily because it came about as a result of a most improbable event: Blumenthal feeling out-anoraked at a food conference. Strange as that seems, it really did happen. At the annual Oxford Symposium on Food and Cookery, he was overwhelmed by presentations on topics as specialist as baby food in the Ming dynasty. When he retired from the hall for some fresh air and to clear his head, he met two men who described themselves as 'food archaeologists'. It was a meeting that confirmed and reawakened his interest in historical food. The eventual result was the beef royal, which nodded back to a classic dish of 1723.

A dish with a contemporary influence also hit the tasting menu in 2007. The 1967 film *Barefoot in the Park* includes a scene in which some unenthusiastic diners are served some Nichi. Although they are warned that, unless they eat the Nichi whole and within a certain timeframe, the taste will be unbearably bitter, the warning is not universally followed. A friend of Blumenthal called Andoni Luis Aduriz commissioned him to create a dish based on this scene, to be added to his book *35mm*, which would be full of cinematically inspired recipes. He created an eel-based dish in tribute to the scene from Neil Simon's comedy and slipped it into the tasting menu at The Fat Duck.

A productive year was completed with the creation of the flaming sorbet, a pudding that, despite being set on fire at the table, did not melt, thanks to its coating of gellan. A multi-sensory effect was created with crackling sound created by dry-ice and scent being created by a variety of means.

With all this activity at The Fat Duck, public interest in the restaurant was rocketing. And it was only going to increase when Blumenthal published a book that revealed the secrets, the history and the recipes of the restaurant. After what was described by the *Guardian* as 'a fierce auction', resulting in an advance of at least £300,000, he sold the idea to Bloomsbury publishers.

The book was nearly three years in the making as Blumenthal once more refused to rush the process and demanded everything was done to his specific demands. The result was astonishing: an extravagant and delightful book that he called *The Big Fat Duck Cookbook*. A weighty, luxurious hardback, it is 528 pages long. The packaging is simple yet elegant: a grey box decorated only with an embossed feather and containing a book in the same grey colour. The Fat Duck logo (cutlery redesigned to represent duck features) is embossed on the cover and the title only appears on the substantial spine. The excited reader opens the book to be bombarded by colour, images and words. Illustrated throughout by fantastic cartoonish images of Blumenthal at work, the book includes a host of recipes, the stories behind the dishes and a potted autobiography of Blumenthal. It seems a cliché, but the reader can almost hear the dishes being sizzled, can almost smell the food as it is served, such is the warmth, richness and enthusiasm of the chef's descriptions.

It is a *very* Blumenthal book: never before has a cookbook so reflected the chef that created it. Naturally, it is full of surprises: a cartoon here, a random-but-related anecdote there. The contents page is not at the front of the book as convention would demand. No, it is in a fold-out, centre-page spread, illustrated by a heady picture of Blumenthal's brain exploding with ideas. He also gives over nearly a fifth of the book to the words of others. A host of scientists and other experts write sections. Yet, while their contributions are important, they all too often lack the charm of Blumenthal who manages to combine attention to detail with humour and chattiness in his sections.

The acknowledgements page reflects Blumenthal's generosity of spirit. It ends with thanks to his family: 'To Zanna for her support, no matter what the sacrifice. The Fat Duck wouldn't have succeeded without her. To Jack, Jessica and Joy for bringing a smile to my face. And to Stephen and Celia for being proud parents.' With luxurious production values, this was not a book that was likely to come cheap and it did not: the RRP was £125.

During the two years he spent writing it, Blumenthal was at home for a little more time. It was then that he discovered just how much of his family's routine he was unaware of, thanks to the demands of his job at the Bray restaurants. Now, as he watched them go about their daily business, he felt like a stranger. 'It was like walking into somebody else's family,' he said. 'They had their own routine of homework, dinner, getting ready for school and, with the exception of my son, all of them love watching *EastEnders*. So I would stand and watch this whole routine which exists without me.' There and then, he vowed to redouble his efforts as a father.

When the results of his writing were finished and the luxurious book was ready to thump on to the shelves (it weighs around five kilograms), there was just one question. What would the critical reception be? William Skidelsky of the *Observer Food Monthly* was an early reviewer, and one who had become very excited about the publication of the book. 'It's here! All week I've been in a state of tremulous anticipation... and now it's landed (or rather thudded) on to my desk: an advanced copy of Heston Blumenthal's massive, epoch-defining, silver ostrich feather-embossed *Fat Duck Cookbook*, which is published by Bloomsbury later this month,' he wrote with palpable joy. 'The latest offerings of Jamie, Nigella and Gordon suddenly seem paltry in comparison. This is the one cookbook that no serious foodie can afford to be without.' So far so good, but would his enthusiasm continue? 'Or is it? One could easily argue that, while it contains plenty of recipes, *The Fat Duck Cookbook* is not really a cookbook at all. Even if you can afford the price tag (and in the current climate that's an ask in itself), how many people are going to summon up the energy and determination to actually cook the recipes in this book? Not only are they fiendishly complex, involving a bamboozling number of stages, but they call for equipment (a dehydrator, a cartouche) that most people won't even have heard of, let alone have to hand.' This was in danger of becoming a roasting for the book, and the words got harsher. 'No, it's safe to say that this is a book that will be more gazed at than cooked from. Its luscious, extravagantly designed pages will for the most part remain unsplattered by specks of foam and liquid nitrogen... In a way, it seems spectacularly out of kilter with the times.'

The *Telegraph* reviewer Xanthe Clay took a novel approach to her review. 'It's a big deal – and we are talking big,' she wrote. 'At 5.4 kilos and the size of a stack of paving slabs, it's not so much a coffee-table book as a coffee table. The book is certainly theatrical. Inside the silver-edged pages, anecdotes from the Fat Duck sit alongside manga-style cartoons of Blumenthal and his alter ego Child Heston.'

The original angle she took for her review involved her trying out one of the recipes in the book. She was stunned by how complicated it was and was only partially pleased with the result of her labours. Of the book itself, her review concluded, 'A laboratory may be a more natural home for Blumenthal's book, but when the paperback comes out I might just put it in the kitchen.'

A better response, but still the write-ups would have made for less than ideal reading for Blumenthal thus far. Surely they would get better? Joanna Heath in *Newsweek* was more visually impressed than pleased with the actual text itself. 'With its comic-book-style illustrations and lovely photographs, the book is truly a work of art,' she purred. 'Still, the recipes are almost comically impossible to reproduce at home – in his jelly of oyster and passion fruit, for example, Blumenthal calls for ingredients such as 170-bloom leaf gelatin and advises cooks to use a spectrometer to measure sugar levels.'

The weight of the book was attracting many comments in the reviews, which might have been frustrating for its author. Vanessa Thorpe and Hannah Gousy wrote in the *Guardian* that, 'if you want to put on a stone (6.3 kilos) in weight, this is the cookbook for you. Retailing at an astonishing £100, Heston Blumenthal's lavish new volume of recipes registers more than 12 pounds on the bathroom scales. And that is without its silver, duck feather-embossed box.' However, having highlighted the 'astonishing' price, they ultimately concluded that the price actually represented a bargain in one sense. 'Yet the book is arguably a democratic move from Britain's most avant-garde gastronome. For £100 you can sample at home the food on the menu at the restaurant that is repeatedly judged the best in Britain, The Fat Duck at Bray in Berkshire. This is a fraction of the cost of an average bill at Blumenthal's triple-Michelin-starred headquarters, famed for its 18-course tasting menu. Perhaps it is a bargain then, assuming that your kitchen is already equipped with an atomiser, a vacuum chamber and a laboratory-style centrifuge.'

With Blumenthal's fame by now international, the overseas press too reviewed *The Big Fat Duck Cookbook*. Betty Hallock of the *Los Angeles Times* wrote, 'This is Fat Duck chef Blumenthal's coming showstopper of a cookbook.' Corey Mintz concluded in Canada's *Toronto*

Star newspaper that *The Big Fat Duck Cookbook* 'straddles the realms of coffee-table art, memoir and confession. *The Big Fat Duck Cookbook* follows this tradition. Flipping through its pages is a tour through an art gallery, with each painting featuring a "How I did it" magician's explanation. It's just a crazy cookbook for crazy cooks.' This was getting better for Blumenthal. Again and again, though, the weight was a source of concentration. Richard Vines of *Bloomberg* told his readers, 'The tome tips the scale at 4.5 kilos (9.9 pounds), making this one of the weightiest cookbooks of the U.K. holiday season.' However, his focus on the weight of the book was turned to Blumenthal's advantage with its final comment: 'It is worth its weight in snails.'

The South African press also took notice, with Dario De Angeli in the *South African Times* saying, 'If food is your life and you live to eat; if you dream about impressing people at your dining table and find your day is incomplete without a visit to your favourite food store, if you want to be inspired; if you want to create in your kitchen, but lack the confidence to do so, then you cannot be without this book.'

Later in the year, Blumenthal received a more considered review, from his long-term associate Jay Rayner. Writing in the *Guardian* in October 2008, Rayner ventured, 'The book of the restaurant is very much more than a compendium of things you can do with interesting ingredients and nice bits of kit. It is a journey into the mind of the man who has done more than almost anybody in Britain to re-engineer the way high-end restaurants approach the knotty business of cooking for us and feeding us.' He explained that the book began with a condensed life-story of the chef. 'Next come the complete Fat Duck recipes, with the glossiest and filthiest of gastro-porn photography. (Who knew the whipping of a pink-spiced pickling foam could look so, well, gynaecological?) These recipes are staggeringly long, involve fiendishly expensive pieces of equipment, are extraordinarily detailed and are probably, for the home cook, completely unmanageable, but that's to miss the point. As Blumenthal himself says: "To change any part of these recipes so that they are more easily achievable would be to compromise – something this book does not do."' Rayner was really 'getting' what Blumenthal and his book were all about. He brought his review to an end by predicting that *The Big Fat Duck Cookbook* would have a considerable influence on the gastronomic globe. 'An awful lot of professional chefs will also buy it, study the science section in detail, examine the recipes and let that influence seep deep into their own cooking,' he wrote. 'Those wrong-headed, appetite-challenged killjoys who are suspicious of what Blumenthal does will regard this as an unfortunate development. As for me, I can only see it as a very good thing indeed.'

At the close of 2008, many publications published round-ups of the year's best books in various genres. *The Big Fat Duck Cookbook* featured in some, including Tom Jaine's culinary book round-up in the *Guardian*. 'The format of *The Big Fat Duck Cookbook* is so overbearing that readers will need a lectern,' he said. 'Handsome, yes; useful, no (I needed vari-focus spectacles to read from the top to the bottom of a single page, so vast was its area).' Elizabeth Luard was far more positive in *The Scotsman*. 'Heston's *The Big Fat Duck Cookbook* weighs in with 1,000 pages at £100 a pop: super-stylish, great info, if that happens to be your bag,' she wrote. 'Which, as it happens, is £20 cheaper than the menu-du-jour at his restaurant in Bray.'

These were better reviews and 2008 saw Blumenthal receive an even greater plaudit as another award was headed his way. *The Fat Duck* was voted the best restaurant in the UK. The *Good Food Guide 2008* now had a top 40, where previous editions had listed the top 10, and Blumenthal's Bray outlet topped the poll, beating the restaurants of Gordon Ramsey and Raymond Blanc. 'Ramsay and Raymond Blanc's restaurants are unmissable experiences, but The Fat Duck has produced truly stunning food this year,' said Elizabeth Carter, editor of the *Guide*. 'Congratulations to Heston Blumenthal for daring to push at the boundaries of modern cooking.'

As for Blumenthal, he was as ever quick to offer credit to others. 'It's a real honour to be voted number one by one of the most respected food guides and a real reflection of how hard the whole team have worked,' he said generously.

In 2009, *The Big Fat Duck Cookbook* was voted Food Book of The Year at the 14th Guild of Food Writers Awards.

He has made no apology for the detail of the recipes, because he is insistent that the book was not to be a watered-down, everyday version of the recipes at the restaurant itself. 'I make no apologies for it not being the

Fat Duck at Home,' said Blumenthal. 'It's not intended to be a book that turns Fat Duck dishes into domestic kitchen fare. The recipes are down-to-the-milligram Fat Duck recipes. All the secrets are given away. There's no "If you can't get foie gras, go and buy yourself chicken livers." Some of these dishes have taken several years to get right – and there may be an ingredient in there without which they will not be the same.' Nor does he offer an excuse for the high price of the book. 'In the UK £40 is a really serious cost barrier for publishers. No chef has ever done a book more than 40 quid. I wanted mine to be more expensive than 40 quid and eventually they accepted it. Then 40 became 50, became 60 and now I think it's at £100. At one point I made the mistake of saying to a publisher: "I don't care how many copies it sells," and I could see their jaw dropping, see them going "Nooooo!"'

A fair few of the reviewers of the book had asked who it was aimed at: domestic cooks, scientists, professional chefs? Blumenthal's answer was certainly honest: 'Me,' he laughed. 'If I'm brutally honest, this is a selfish piece of work. Of course I want to sell as many copies as possible, but it does have its own barriers built in. The idea is that, because there's so much information in there, you'll still be discovering new things in it in five years. We all have the ability to leave a legacy in some shape or form. The whole aesthetic of the book was to encapsulate my approach to food.'

All the same, a smaller version is in the offing. 'I actually have agreed with the publishers that, after a year, we're going to do a £35 version,' he said. 'So the book will get scaled down; it'll still have all the information in there, but it will just be a smaller book, so the accessibility comes in at that point.' He was not happy with all the responses to his recipes in the book. 'To hear those comments that [our style of cuisine] is dehumanising cooking, and reducing it to a test-tube, people are completely misunderstanding it. If you really wanted to be a purist about it, man should only ever cook over fire, not use anything electrical.'

Of the weight of the book, Blumenthal reveals that it could have been a far heavier proposition if he had had his way. 'There are about 120,000 to 140,000 words of text right now,' he had said during the writing of it. 'Loads of text. We've got 700-something pages, but, with the weight of paper we want, we can only have about 450 to 500. And the book is in three sections: The first section is sort of biographical; the second will be 50-odd recipes and sub-recipes; then there's the section on science. We'll have info on ice cream science, meat science, etc., and a bit on equipment and ingredients; then there are 18 pieces by different academics (including a hydrocolloid specialist, the head of the UK Synaesthesia Association, somebody who works on pain and pleasure mechanisms, a perfumier, a flavourist, etc.). I'm sort of writing through those sections about how I translate the science into my work. I don't want to leave anything out, but I might have to reduce the text in that third section and have it be like a reference book. But in those first two sections I wanted to try and have a lot of white page space, and we've got two photographers and an illustrator too.'

He was also continuing with his newspaper writing.

Having previously written a column for the *Guardian*, Blumenthal wrote for *The Sunday Times*. In one such column he wrote about his old favourite, the Lewis Carroll novel *Alice in Wonderland*. 'Alice has been a favourite book of mine for a while,' he revealed. 'I love the way she makes reason in a completely unreasonable world. I think cooking is like going down a rabbit hole into a wonderland – the sense of discovery, the way that things are not quite as they seem.'

Writing about steak, he returned to his childhood. 'As far as I was concerned as a child, steak was for grown-ups,' he said. 'It was what you graduated to from burgers. This was partly due to economics: meat was very expensive in Britain in the 1970s and the top-quality cut you need for steak became the province of the restaurant business – part of a big night out.'

He also wrote about more surprisingly simple dishes such as cheese on toast, albeit with a Blumenthal twist, of course.

Through all this media work, he became more and more famous. Again, he is not one to complain about the 'pitfalls of fame' as some do. Indeed, he is pleasantly surprised by what celebrity has to offer him. 'I do get stopped in the street,' he said. 'But I suppose if it's all right for a chef to write a book it's all right to do TV. To be honest, I was very surprised by the positive response.'

New recipes, awards, a *Sunday Times* column and book sales, 2008 had been a phenomenal year for Blumenthal. However, in 2009, his level of fame was to rocket as he became the focal point of new television programmes and a very public embarrassment.

CHAPTER SIX

LITTLE BY LITTLE

The television screens of Britain have been treated to an astonishing amount of cooking shows in recent years, many of which straddled the reality-television genre. Jamie Oliver fronted *Jamie's School Dinners* on Channel 4 in 2005 in an attempt to improve the food that schoolchildren eat and his show became a national talking point with its attacks on Turkey Twizzlers. Gordon Ramsay took on failing restaurants in *Ramsay's Kitchen Nightmares* on Channel 4. Meanwhile, over on ITV, celebrities competed on his *Hell's Kitchen*, a culinary take on the well-worn *Big Brother* format. These were guaranteed winners in the ratings battle and soon Channel 4 were looking for their next big show. For this, they turned to Blumenthal. They had done wonders with Oliver the likely lad and Ramsay the alpha-male swearer. Now it was time, it seemed, for the geek.

In March 2008, Blumenthal signed a two-year deal with

Channel 4 and the first series to come from the deal propelled him into the consciousness of millions of new people. It was a concept to whet the appetite of television viewers. Heston Blumenthal, one of the greatest cooks in the world, the creator of the famous Fat Duck tasting menu, was to take on ailing roadside restaurant chain Little Chef and the whole thing would be filmed for a television documentary mini-series. A Channel 4 source said, 'It is something out of a mad dream – a bit like Willy Wonka meets Kathy's Cafe from *EastEnders*. One of the planet's most innovative cooks will be passing on his skills to a roadside diner. Instead of the usual fry-ups, customers could get something weird like fish ice cream.' The potential scope of the series was enormous: motorway dining might never be the same again.

This was quite a prospect and immediately caught the notice of the printed press. Rachel Dixon, writing in the *Guardian*, asked, 'Who'd have thought it? Heston Blumenthal, a chef who has built a career around an obsessive quest for perfection, is trying to tart up Little Chef. He's going to have quite a job on his hands. Still, three hour-long TV programmes should just about do the trick. No, hang on – apparently it will take him that long to sort out one lucky branch of Little Chef, leaving just another 185 to go. Now that sounds more like Heston.'

The man himself accepted that it might seem to outsiders a strange project for him to take on. 'Was I mad to say "yes"?' asked Blumenthal. 'You might think that, but doesn't everyone have fond memories of what the Little

Chef used to be from every holiday drive? People really wanted to eat in them. I wanted to see if I could do anything to help. There's a contrast between this so-called "molecular gastronomy" that people always talk about when they talk about my cooking and a restaurant where, when I first walked in, there wasn't a single pot or pan in the kitchen,' he added. 'The Little Chef's staff weren't chefs, they were people trained to do a certain job. I genuinely wanted to see what we could do – but I also never wanted to turn the place into "Little Heston's".'

He admitted that many people close to him doubted whether this was a wise project for him to take on. 'When I said I was doing this, people said, "Why on earth are you doing that?" If I'm totally honest, my excitement going into this was too ideological. I thought I'd get a perfumier in, a lighting technologist, sound engineers. It was like climbing Everest when I should have been taking one step. The practicalities of running a place from 7am to 7pm, seven days a week involved three shifts of staff – that's 24 chefs per day. The cost of that meant we couldn't do it without driving the price of the dishes up and it was key that we kept the menu about the same price.' As to why he thought the chain had previously suffered, he was clear. 'There's been a big increase in roadside cafes and restaurants and they didn't respond well to the competition. Now we're taking it back to the basics. The sausage recipe has been developed from scratch, the recipes have been developed from scratch and it's all been done with excitement.'

The show was called *Big Chef Takes on Little Chef* and

was broadcast on Channel 4 in January 2009, less than 12 months after the network first signed him up. It made for brilliant viewing. Episode one began with the contrast between Blumenthal's world and the world of the Little Chef chain clearly spelled out. With operatic music in the background, aerial shots of Bray were shown, together with footage of Blumenthal's chefs preparing lunch at The Fat Duck. It was idyllic and sophisticated, a world away from the roadside chain he was about to take on. He then took a break with his staff in the garden of the venue and discussed with them their Little Chef experiences as customers. Jocky, one of his head chefs, said he remembered going there for treats as a child.

Blumenthal said, 'I went once when I was about 20, when I was going to a wedding in Norfolk.' It was a contrast to earlier interviews in which he had spoken at length of his memories of childhood visits to Little Chef.

The cameras followed him back into the kitchen, where he explained some of the more adventurous tasting-menu dishes. He talked the crew through the Sounds of the Sea dish. He revealed, 'We've had, I'd say, four or five people actually crying when eating this dish.'

And yet he was excited by the challenge ahead of him at the roadside chain. 'Little Chef is the most iconic roadside restaurant chain in Britain,' he said. 'I am proud to be British. To have the challenge is a big honour, if I get it right that will be a fantastic achievement.'

The action then moved to the Popham branch of Little Chef, where Blumenthal was going to be based during the challenge ahead. The staff were all obviously apprehensive of what lay ahead for them once Blumenthal arrived. 'Heston... can't remember his surname,' said one waiter when asked what he knew about Blumenthal. 'He makes funny ice cream.'

Two of his colleagues were shown having a bemused discussion about Blumenthal's famous bacon and egg ice-cream recipe. 'But that's hot and cold,' said one. The restaurant manager spelled out the dilemma that would face Blumenthal for the entire task. 'I'm not sure people are ready for snail porridge in Little Chef – they weren't ready for muesli,' he laughed.

Blumenthal's first appointment of the show was at the chain's head office in Sheffield. En route, he pulled off at a Little Chef just off the A38 motorway in Derbyshire. He sat down and perused the extensive menu which offered up to 70 different dishes. Noting that different countries' dishes were featured on the plentiful menu, he said, 'This is the menu of a company in a panic.' He then ordered off the menu, so he could try some of the food. First up, he tucked into the mega-mix grill. He found some of the meat very tough and told the camera, 'I think it's going to take me as long to chew this one piece as it did for this dish to arrive.' Turning to the chicken on his plate, he complained of its blandness. Next up, his slightly confused waitress brought him the famous Little Chef Olympic breakfast. 'Well, it is massive,' he said as it arrived in front of him. The quality did not impress him as much as the quantity, however. 'I think more of it has come from the baker than the actual farmer,' he said of the sausage he ate. Turning to the unappetising-looking scrambled eggs, he was scornful. 'It's rubbery,' he said in disgust. 'It doesn't taste of anything. That's amazing.' The scrambled eggs had been cooked in a microwave, a million miles from the preparatory methods of The Fat Duck.

As he continued on his journey, he explained how he hoped to relaunch the famous chain. 'The British public once fell in love with Little Chef,' he said. 'I grew up in the Seventies and it was the place to go as a kid. That's what I want to do: to put that excitement back.'

On arrival in Sheffield, he was greeted by Ian Pegler, the newly appointed chief executive of Little Chef. A former executive at M&S and Dixons, he had also worked at Forte in the early 1990s. A lively, grey-haired man, he was to prove an entertaining character in the series, although not necessarily in the way he might have hoped. Blumenthal got straight down to business, telling Pegler that, having eaten at the Derbyshire branch and examined the menu, he demanded a sweeping change. 'I'm absolutely adamant that that menu has to go,' he said, 'the whole menu.'

Pegler replied, 'Heston, I'm prepared for you to do anything you like – seriously. What I want you to come up with is a taste explosion in everything that you do.'

Blumenthal began to discuss the financial side of the Little Chef operation, mentioning profits, but Pegler wouldn't be distracted. He told his new chef, 'I want you to come up with the weirdest, wackiest whatever and then funnel it down to a commercial product that you know will wow the public.'

Blumenthal tried to return to finances, asking Pegler what Little Chef's gross profit currently was.

'I'm not prepared to say that on air,' said Pegler, looking very uncomfortable.

Blumenthal was shocked. 'You're not prepared to say it?' he asked, bemused.

In his car, after the meeting had ended, he was crestfallen. 'I've come away with more questions than answers and that's really worrying,' he said. He reiterated how disappointing he had found the food he had eaten in Derbyshire, with the egg and the coffee coming in for particularly scathing criticism. He also didn't seem to be overwhelmed in his encounter with Pegler, in contrast to the mood of the chief executive himself, who explained that he felt they had 'an instant chemistry'.

Blumenthal went on to visit a series of Little Chef restaurants to try to understand how they worked. He was given a trainee badge and introduced to the staff. He was surprised that the kitchen didn't have a single pan, which explained why the microwave was used to scramble the eggs. He tried to scramble eggs on a griddle, but failed as he was unable to control the heat.

After driving to the north-east of England, he visited an eerily empty branch. He was stunned by how unpopular it was. 'The breakfast rush is more like a breakfast ghost town,' he said, wide-eyed.

During a second meeting with Pegler, Blumenthal began to experience some of the chief executive's business talk. 'What I want you to do is to think as wide as you possibly can,' he told the chef. 'You can take this core product and just explode it.'

Blumenthal felt that not only was he being asked to perform tricks, but also that they were ones that cancelled each other out. 'He's asking me to pull a rabbit out of the hat,' he told the camera back in the BMW. 'He's not caring about the dishes or the ingredients. He's caring about the fireworks that you put on top. It's just another example of "Let's paint over the cracks."' Noting that the chief executive seemed to expect adventurous food that nonetheless did not alienate existing Little Chef customers and that used expensive ingredients on a small budget, he concluded, '[Pegler] is contradicting himself.'

Blumenthal nonetheless took up the challenge, which he defined as 'To reinvent British classics for the 21st century'.

In the kitchen in Bray, he developed some new ideas which he hoped did just that. First up, he put together a traditional hotpot that included oysters, thyroid and tongue alongside the meat. A modern potato soup, which would harness the flavour of buttered jacket potato, was also conjured up, alongside a scrambled-egg dish with smoked salmon and the essence of Earl Grey tea.

With the wind in his sails from some successful kitchen magic, Blumenthal phoned Pegler again to question him further on the company finances. The chief executive did his best to fudge the issue and evade Blumenthal's direct questions. In the end, the line went dead, with Pegler seemingly having hung up on the chef. Blumenthal burst out laughing and looked on with shock. He phoned straight back and found that Pegler's line went to voicemail. 'If I don't hear back from you in the next half-an-hour, that's going to send some very serious signals to me,' he told the answering machine. 'OK? I look forward to hearing from you.' He then looked on in shock again that Pegler appeared to have hung up on him.

But he soon met up with Pegler again, who introduced him to the Popham branch, just outside Basingstoke, which would be his home for the task. 'It's certainly less depressing than some others I've seen,' said Blumenthal, damning it with faint praise.

'Well, thanks for that crumb of comfort,' quipped Pegler.

The first stage of the task was simple: the Popham branch would be divided in two so customers could decide whether they preferred the existing Little Chef menu or whether they dared to go with Blumenthal's updated version.

Ahead of the challenge, Heston was introduced to the staff, who included branch manager Michael Cook. He was polite on meeting Blumenthal. However, he later confided to the crew that he feared the chef would 'make us a laughing stock by putting something random on the menu like rabbit-flavoured jelly, or something like that'.

Before the challenge began, Blumenthal brought his two head chefs to the branch to garner their impressions of the place. It made for slightly uncomfortable viewing as his colleagues didn't disguise their opinions of the place. 'You're kidding me?' said Jocky repeatedly. 'Seriously? Is this for real?'

Their table had ripped fabric on the chairs and they

spotted a spider on the ceiling. 'At least we won't be dining alone,' joked his colleague.

Sam Wollaston, reviewing the episode in the *Guardian*, quipped of Blumenthal: 'It's hard to tell if he's disgusted or if he's thinking: "Hmmm, I could do something with that – apple spider with fly scream.'

One of Heston's chefs ordered a Hawaiian burger. When it arrived, he complained, 'The burger is so dry.' Blumenthal vowed to remove the dish from the menu.

Tom Sutcliffe focused on this scene in his review of the episode in the *Independent*. 'Channel 4, at least, knew precisely what it was getting into by pairing off Britain's most experimental chef with one of the country's most predictable chains,' he began. 'It had signed up for an effectively unloseable each-way bet. Either Blumenthal brought it off, in which case we could marvel at the coming of age of the British palate, or the collision of cultures would turn explosive, in which case they got three episodes of argy-bargy and quite a bit of snickering at the yawning gap between a Michelin-starred menu and one that has to have photographs on it for customers who can't read. What it may not have reckoned with was how sour a taste this might leave, as you watched the culinarily-privileged mocking a form of social deprivation.'

In a reversal of roles, Blumenthal invited Little Chef boss Pegler and his team to The Hinds Head so they could sample the dishes he was planning to feature on his menu for the challenge ahead. The mint and pea soup (which had replaced the potato soup in his plans) left them unimpressed. 'The soup is not quite as I had expected; it didn't layer as I hoped,' said Pegler. When they turned to the hotpot, the chief executive's verdict was scarcely kinder. 'It's interesting how it coats the roof of your mouth,' he said, adding he thought it was too salty.

After the meeting, Pegler spoke to the crew, saying, 'I want fire and brimstone, blue-sky thinking,' before he headed home.

Blumenthal was plainly disappointed at the encounter.

It was then the day of the challenge, in which the Popham Little Chef would be divided in two and Blumenthal's menu would go head to head with the existing one. He was in bullish mood on the morning of the task. 'We're going to throw down the gauntlet,' Blumenthal declared. 'I'm going to show Ian that his menu is basically rubbish. I'm going to win.'

His confidence was not matched by the reality. On a busy day in Popham, it took an agonising 90 minutes before two customers chose his menu. They then disappeared before the food was even ready. The camera crew were there to capture the thoughts of Little Chef's customers on the new Blumenthal menu. 'I was a little bit thrown by the scrambled eggs,' said one, while another thought, 'It's a little bit poncy. It's not the environment where you expect that sort of food.'

The verdict was little better from Pegler, who phoned to tell Blumenthal that he felt what he was offering was not exciting enough. 'I could get the same food from any other celebrity chef,' he told him.

After the call ended, Blumenthal was undaunted. 'I'm just going to carry on, actually.'

And yet the culture clash between the Bray bunch and the Popham people continued. Fat Duck chef Ashley seemingly offended branch manager Cook, who snapped, 'Don't wind me up, I really hate that. Don't think you're better than me, because you're not.'

Later, the pair had another confrontation in the garden. 'Little Chef is not about fancy food,' said Cook. 'It's about quick food, on the table – in and out.'

Ashley felt that Cook was overestimating how long it took for their dishes to be prepared. 'That's a total exaggeration of how long it takes to do that,' he said of Cook's assessment.

The branch manager later told the crew that he felt Blumenthal's team were looking down on him and Little Chef. Blumenthal was horrified by how badly his menu had performed in the challenge, and was hurt by the remarks of the customers that what he was offering was 'poncy'. 'I didn't grow up eating lobster and caviar, I'm a normal bloke,' he said. However, he accepted he would have to go back to the drawing board and create a new menu.

Pegler ended the episode by explaining he was producing a brief for Blumenthal, who he wanted 'to think out of the box and this blue-sky thinking'.

The media was abuzz with discussion of the opening episode. Andrew Billen reviewed it for *The Times*: 'But if Little Chef came out looking rather plucky, Big Chef emerged looking deranged. Meticulously-deranged cooking is Blumenthal's speciality, of course, along with his molten arctic roll and sound of the sea fish dish (served with an iPod in a shell). Not for nothing is the kitchen at the back of The Fat Duck in Berkshire called "experimental". But deranged experimentation is not what your Little Chef customers are looking for. Those few in a Hampshire branch who plumped for his offerings looked aggrieved. Lancashire hotpot with oyster and thyroid? Even the vague recognition that this was "traditional" and "English" was no excuse.' He concluded, 'Poor Blumenthal. How he must rue the day he left the BBC which had politely indulged his experiments and laughed silently.'

Susan Smilie was more positive in her review for the *Guardian*: 'While I'm sure he doesn't mind the publicity, I don't think the comparison is fair,' she said. 'Heston isn't someone I suspect of hamming it up for the camera and while it's easy to label him poncy (it's telling that the comments from punters about the "poncy" food affect him far more than Pegler's management-speak), he comes across as a hard-working chef who genuinely wants to please people with food, whether they're in The Fat Duck or, well, a Little Chef. He holds his hands up to the fact that he's failed on this count – a tough thing for any perfectionist to handle – and he doesn't lay the blame elsewhere.' She added, 'It's not Blumenthal's style to shout about how he's transforming the nation's diet – he's not setting himself up as another campaigning chef and all the more credit to him for that. But it's plain to see he cares about people eating well; the Little Chef revamp should be an important step in achieving that.'

It had been an engrossing opening episode to the series. Numerous tensions had been created which promised much fun in episode two. Would it live up to expectations?

The task for episode two was clear: Blumenthal had to reinvent the famous Little Chef Olympic breakfast, which had been a star of the chain's menu for three decades. He was under no illusion as to the scale of the challenge. 'If I fail, it could be complete humiliation,' he said. Despite the disappointment of his first task in the previous edition, he was determined to bounce back, 'because I feel very attached to this whole project now, because I take it very personally, I ain't gonna give up,' he said. 'I can't give up. I really want to help Little Chef. I want to get this menu right and I'm even prepared to go back to the drawing board.

Blumenthal set out what was at stake for his relaunch. The breakfasts at Little Chef constitute half of their sales and had become, he noted, 'their jewel in the crown'. So, to put into practice his relaunch, he would need to identify one chef who could take control of the project in Popham. To this end, he auditioned Little Chef staff from across the UK in the hope of uncovering a gem. The first task he set them was to cook scrambled eggs – using a pan. Little Chef sold 5,000 scrambled-egg meals per week but he wanted the dish to step up a gear. The results were far from ideal. First he found a dry offering, cooked by an employee named Anne England who had been at Little Chef for an amazing 30 years. Then he sampled another attempt, which was soggy. 'This one looks like it's gone for a swim,' sighed Blumenthal.

Next up, he gave his auditionees a fresh bream fish and

vegetables. He then allotted them just 45 minutes to knock the ingredients together into a tasty dish. Here there was even more disappointment for Blumenthal. Many of the fishes at the end of the process were woefully undercooked. 'They're not cooks,' he said, shaking his head as the reality of his challenge became clear in his mind. 'They're not trained chefs. That's a bombshell.'

He clearly had not unearthed a hidden gem who could take control of the preparation of his Olympic breakfast relaunch in the kitchen. So, he chose an unconventional route. Anne England had performed particularly badly in the auditions. Therefore, he felt, if he could train her to put out his new breakfast, then he could confidently claim that any Little Chef kitchen could manage the same. England was astonished when he phoned her and said that he was appointing her to his Olympic relaunch in Popham. 'If I can train you, I can train anyone,' he told her. It was a maverick plan and the reality of the gamble he had taken was not lost on him. 'I've officially employed the worst cook I've ever come across,' he said, 'and the success of my breakfast menu depends on her.'

England, too, was aware of what was at stake. When she visited his kitchen in Bray, she said of The Fat Duck, 'It's a world apart of difference.'

She was shown some of the tricks she would be asked to use when preparing the new breakfast, from brushing tomatoes with fresh thyme oil to drizzling sherry vinegar over the fried eggs. England was not brimming with confidence that she could help introduce this new culture to the Little Chef staff. 'I wouldn't put any money on him pulling this off,' she said.

As a test run, she was asked to serve the breakfast for Blumenthal and his team. She flapped under pressure and allowed some small mistakes to make undue knocks in her confidence. As she finally served up, she was in such a state she couldn't even talk straight. 'I'm so demolarised [sic],' she said.

Meanwhile, Blumenthal was looking beyond the breakfast issue and finalising what would form the basis of his new main menu. His first attempt had been mired in contradiction: Pegler's view was that the new food was not imaginative enough, while the Little Chef customers had complained that it was too 'poncy'. It was a difficult balance for Blumenthal to strike and he concluded that the only way to manage it was to perform some market research. Which dishes did the Great British public most like?

Heston took to the streets of England and the early results included a substantial vote for chips, prawn cocktails and pate. There were also votes aplenty for liver and onion, lamb shank and fish and chips. He had lots to think about as a result. And yet, as he travelled round the country, he continued to be prickled by the 'poncy' allegations that had been thrown at him at the start of his mini-series. As he stared out of a train window, he reflected on how mistaken his public image might be. 'It's like people think I'm living in a gastronomic food bubble, out of touch with so-called ordinary people. But I didn't grow up posh. I didn't live off caviar as a kid. I'm a normal bloke, yeah? I'm a normal bloke.' The experience of participating in the show had made him aware of how some of the public viewed him, and given him food for thought about his public image. 'Those comments of it being poncy, fussy, complicated, it's like being kicked in the stomach,' he added. 'I don't consider myself to be a poncy person.'

As an early test for his new breakfast, Blumenthal and his team pitched up outside an England rugby match with a stall punting his breakfast to the fans. His was alongside another selling breakfasts and boasting of its best café in Britain 2008 award. It also included baked beans in its line-up, an ingredient Blumenthal had campaigned hard to omit from his relaunched Olympic breakfast. Here was another challenge for him. 'If we can outsell them,' he declared, looking at the opposition and their proud banner, 'then we've cracked it.'

He received good feedback from those customers who chose his outlet for their food, with one man claiming it had been 'the best breakfast I've ever had'. But when it came to totting up the scores, his rivals next door had outsold Blumenthal by 88 to 65, largely, it seemed, because they offered baked beans. 'I might have to concede on the baked beans,' he sighed. What helped to make up his mind was his feeling that new recruit Anne England, who was a strong advocate of baked beans, would only be completely committed to the task of introducing the breakfast at Popham if they were on the menu.

Pegler was continuing to entertain viewers in his own way.

He told the camera that most celebrities he had worked with were disingenuous, and that a memorable exception was 'an actress, I can't remember her name… anyway, doesn't matter. I think Heston is a really genuine guy, and I'd like to be his friend.' As he read the proposed new main menu that Blumenthal had put together as a result of his market research, he said he enjoyed 'moments of joy'.

Despite the praise, Blumenthal was becoming increasingly sceptical about why he had really been invited on to the programme. 'Do they really want to do this?' he wondered to the camera of his new menu. 'Or are they just seeing it as a great opportunity to get some marketing for Little Chef?'

Meanwhile, it was time for Anne England to oversee the introduction of the new breakfast in the Popham branch. Here she represented a plucky underdog, sent in by Blumenthal to convert her colleagues to his way of working. As Ashley told her in the drive to Popham, 'Don't let them talk back, you're one of us now.'

The early signs were promising: when the Popham staff sampled the food, they were impressed, and even the branch manager was delighted. 'Really nice,' said Cook.

Blumenthal was more confident than he had been throughout his Little Chef experience. But then came news that disappointed him again. England told him that a new main menu was being launched nationally by Little Chef the following week. When he examined it, he noticed it included a lot of the dishes he had proposed to Pegler that he would eventually introduce himself. He was furious. Not only did he suspect afresh that his role was purely to provide cheap marketing for them, but he also feared that dishes which he had no part in putting together would be linked to him. 'Do you think they're just seeing this as a marketing opportunity?' he wondered out loud once again.

Blumenthal was worried about the direction the enterprise was taking and, armed with many unanswered questions, he tracked Pegler down so he could confront him in person. He eventually found him at a Holiday Inn hotel, where he was attending a corporate conference. His direct approach seemed to take the Little Chef chief executive quite by surprise. He told him he was aware of the new menu, and asked, 'Why didn't you tell me about that?'

Pegler appeared incredibly uncomfortable during the scene. He kept looking around and asked the crew to turn the camera off. When the TV audience rejoined the action, Blumenthal had asked that Little Chef commit to rolling out his new breakfast beyond Popham to at least four more branches within the following three months. It seemed as though the two differing attitudes had found some common ground – at least for the time being.

Meanwhile, back at Popham, England was preparing to introduce the new breakfast. She suspected that some of Blumenthal's embellishments might go missing once the pressure of the cooking got under way on the day. 'When you're busy, you're not going to pipette,' she said. 'That corner is going to be cut.'

Branch manager Cook was also feeling a little less optimistic. 'We're not chefs,' he said, adding, 'Duck à la banana we're not.'

The new breakfast was to be given a two-day trial and Blumenthal was under no illusions as to what was at stake. If he could not make a success of his breakfast at Popham, what chance did he have of it being introduced nationwide? What chance, come to that, would he have of his main menu issue being resolved? It was all or nothing time. 'Today is the most important day,' he said sombrely. 'My whole reputation rests on this morning and tomorrow morning.'

On day one, he oversaw what was going on as England took control of the kitchen. The early signs were good, as customers offered positive feedback on the new breakfast, including one who awarded high marks on an official feedback card. On day two, England was to be left in sole charge of the kitchen. However, when it came to her expected arrival time, there was no sign of her. She was still in her bed and breakfast, and said she was quitting. 'I'm fed up,' she explained. 'I won't be laughed at. Everybody who knows me knows that.' She had clashed with another cook the previous day and the episode appeared to have dented her confidence. She presented herself to Blumenthal and, much to his disappointment, told him, 'I'm quitting, I'm going home – asap.'

It was clearly something that affected Blumenthal deeply. He would need to use all his management skills to sort this out. Could he talk England round and get her back to Popham? Or would the entire project collapse as a result of her resignation?

He pointed out her importance to his venture, telling

England, 'This whole project rests on you doing this breakfast.' He continued to work sensitively with her, attempting to refuel her drained confidence levels.

Finally, she agreed to return to Popham and run the show. They embraced to seal the conversation and Blumenthal joked about how testing he was finding his Little Chef experience. 'Just every single day there's something,' he said with comedic despair.

England returned to Popham and, although some of the staff were indeed struggling with the pipettes and other flourishes, she oversaw another successful morning that saw takings ten per cent higher than they had been prior to the introduction of Blumenthal's breakfast. He was quick to give the credit to his newest recruit, saying of England, 'I'm really proud of Anne.'

He could be proud of himself, too, as the customers were full of praise once more for his improved breakfast. 'If I knew this was what I was going to get, I would definitely stop,' said one.

Branch manager Cook was thrilled with the praise that was coming their way. 'We haven't had that for a few years,' he told Blumenthal, who replied, 'It's fantastic, isn't it?' The chef was also under no illusions about how close he had come to failure: 'The wheels nearly fell off.' However, he had made it work.

The episode was due a happy ending, but there was still more drama to come. Blumenthal was scheduled to meet with Pegler and was in ebullient mood as he prepared for their encounter. His agenda for the meeting was simple: 'I need a guarantee of this breakfast roll-out,' he said. 'If he doesn't agree to this, why are we busting our guts?'

The meeting was as nail-biting as its build-up suggested it would be, as the two men stood their ground and argued their respective points. 'So are you saying you don't want to put this new breakfast in?' asked Blumenthal. But the meeting failed to elicit the response that he needed. When no promise on the breakfast roll-out was forthcoming, he walked out, telling Pegler, 'That's it, I've had enough now.'

After his walkout, Blumenthal was in defiant mood. 'Until they change their mind, this project is going no further,' he told the camera. 'We're downing tools. I'm walking away.' Could this be the end of the line?

The discord between Blumenthal and Pegler had not been resolved when episode three began. However, it was clear that the chef was not going to drop the project. 'My relationship with Ian has completely broken down,' he said. 'But I've realised there's no way I can walk away from this. Little Chef is an iconic brand. It's part of the national fabric. I've put too much time, stress and effort into this to walk away.' He had commissioned food companies to mass-produce the recipes he was proposing for his main menu and, along with his head chef Ashley, he tested them in the experimental kitchen in Bray. The results were often disappointing: he compared a curry to a suntan lotion, so strong in coconut was the taste. Ashley told him that the company working on their cheesecake recipe had not even delivered a sample, but had offered to send a photograph instead, much to

Blumenthal's despair. 'I told them pictures are no good,' said Ashley. 'A picture I can't eat.'

The pressure was building on Blumenthal and he feared that the mathematics of what he was up against might be insurmountable. 'These companies are massive,' he sighed. 'Trying to get anything out of them in anything less than a year is out of the question and we're trying to do 30 or 40 dishes in less than a month.' There was more bad news when his novel egg-preparation plan appeared to have gone awry too. 'We banked our whole scrambled egg and omelette on this technique,' he said, flicking a segment of almost plastic-looking egg. 'That is not breakfast.'

Ever the perfectionist and tinkerer, Blumenthal was beginning to realise that, with just weeks to go before his menu was expected, he might have to change his way of working. 'If I don't compromise, there ain't going to be anything on the menu,' he shrugged. 'There has to be a compromise somewhere, otherwise we're going to reopen with nothing and then I would have failed in every single way possible.'

But the menu was just part of what he had to concentrate on. In addition, part of his brief was to redesign the interior of the Popham branch. Manager Cook was cautiously optimistic over what this might lead to. 'I'm slightly concerned but I think Little Chef is ready for a bit of change,' he said.

He joined Blumenthal in a tour of the branch, taking in all the imperfections and issues to be addressed in the redesign. The tables, curtains and crockery came in for particular criticism.

Looking to the ugly ceiling, Blumenthal quipped, 'I'm going to keep the ceiling tiles, because I think they're a real design feature.'

Cook burst out laughing and said, 'I hope you're taking the piss, because they are vile, aren't they?'

Turning to the kitchen, his ambition was simple: 'All of that is going,' he said, sweeping his hand across the entire vista, 'the lot.'

Barry then showed Blumenthal his worn, discoloured uniform and asked if as part of the redesign they could get new ones. 'It did come in blue, eight years ago,' he said.

The man given the task of making the redesign happen was Ab Rogers. Having left school at 16 as a trained carpenter, Rogers had since become a renowned designer. He was given just a third of the budget he would normally be awarded to redesign a restaurant of the scale of the Popham Little Chef.

Meanwhile, Blumenthal sat down on a table and once more fretted about how behind the project was. 'We're 20 per cent done on the menu, and that scares the crap out of me,' he said. He was still making small changes to the menu, including the steak and ale pie. As the series' narrator said, 'Being Heston, he's still making tweaks.'

The next task for him was to train the waiting staff to be able to provide the level of service that he demanded. Blumenthal has long advocated the importance of good service and he weighed up the scale of the task ahead, describing the waiting team at Popham as 'a mixed bag'. He continued, 'Some are more motivated than others, some look like they don't even want to be there. I need to get them motivated, excited. I want to make them feel like it's their restaurant. And, when that happens, Little Chef will have something that none of its competitors have – great service.'

To this end, the entire waiting staff and branch manager of Popham were invited to Bray, to The Hinds Head, where he gave them a pep talk. 'You guys are going to be the flag-bearers for my new menu, and you're going to be the flag-bearers for the whole Little Chef chain,' he said. They laughed nervously, before Blumenthal told them he was quite serious. 'You seven are going to set the tone for 180 Little Chefs. So that's what you've got on your shoulders.'

His challenge to them was that the following day they would do the service at The Hinds Head. There, they would be expected to provide the high level of service that its patrons demanded. A key part of this was in-depth knowledge of how the dishes were prepared, so customers' questions could be answered. Blumenthal spent the afternoon explaining to them the intricacies of the dishes on The Hinds Head menu, including the soup and pie. Afterwards, he summed up the challenge that lay ahead for his new staff: 'It's all very well them enjoying the food and having a laugh but tomorrow they're going to be serving my food, in my pub, to my guests and I cannot and will not let them give bad service.' He tested them on the ingredients and preparation of the dishes. He asked chef Barry what was in the chicken and ham pie, to which Barry replied, naturally enough, 'Chicken and ham.' It was a similar story when Blumenthal asked another chef, Jason, what went into the mashed potato soup. 'Erm... potatoes,' answered Jason.

'They fell flat,' said Blumenthal afterwards. 'They've got an awful long way to go.'

Jason predicted that he would not be able to sleep that night, such were his nerves about the following day's service at The Hinds Head. Cook, meanwhile, was worried about Barry too. 'He's like my son,' he explained. The team decided to test each other at the hotel, in the hope of sharpening up their memories. Cook was again protective of Barry, arguing that Blumenthal had been too strict with him. The team were nervous about the challenge ahead, as was Blumenthal who would be mortified if he felt his Hinds Head customers were given less than perfect service.

Blumenthal watched over them the following day as they performed the service. Jason began nervously and a pair of customers complained that he had not asked them what type of mineral water they wanted, and that he was insufficiently helpful with their coats. They then asked about the ingredients of several dishes. Despite some agonising pauses, Jason managed to get all his answers out correctly, much to Blumenthal's delight. 'Bless him, he was so nervous,' said the chef. 'It was literally like willing your kid on at school to win the egg and spoon race.'

Blumenthal personally praised Barry, telling him, 'You've done brilliantly well.' He also complimented Michael, whom he felt took a definite lead of the team, all of whom were applauded by Blumenthal and his customers at the end of the service.

Although good service is paramount to Blumenthal, it is worth noting here that he does not subscribe fully to the maxim that 'the customer is always right'. 'If somebody doesn't like a dish, you try to give them something they will like,' he has said, 'but if a customer tells a member of staff to piss off that cannot be tolerated.' There is a limit. Likewise, there were definite 'no-nos' in the behaviour of the waiters themselves. Blumenthal lists three pet peeves of his when he is a customer in a restaurant. 'One: When a waiter points too closely at your food – you know, when they explain the dish or direction to eat it, but they almost touch your plate. Two: waiters that I have never met before who touch your back or your arm in a familiar way. Three: constant, "How is everything, how was it?" questions during the meal.' It is safe to say that no waiter of his, be it at Little Chef, The Fat Duck or The Hinds Head, should commit any of these faux pas.

Next up in his Little Chef experience was a meeting with the boss man himself, Ian Pegler, whom he wanted to sample the dishes he proposed for his Little Chef main menu, and with whom he wanted to talk budgets. Among these dishes was a chilli con carne. 'It looks like Mrs Pegler's chilli,' he said before tasting it. When he did, he said 'That pokes you in the eye with the cumin,' and asked Blumenthal to make it a little stronger. On the costings, the pair were not so united. Pegler declared that no dishes should be much more than £10, but Blumenthal explained that one of them might need a price closer to £18.50. It was far more than the chain would usually charge for any of their food.

Meanwhile, the refit was coming to an end at Popham and the stock was arriving. As the kitchen was finished, Blumenthal cooked different steaks in it to decide which type to put on the menu. He had still not printed the menu, despite its expected launch the following day. 'I am worried,' he said. 'Yeah, I'm very worried.'

As it was, the dishes were still being photographed for the menu late into the evening, with Ashley on hand to sure that things ran smoothly.

Blumenthal, at the same time, was crunching figures with his financial manager, trying to get the sale price of the dishes as close to the elusive sub-£10 barrier as possible. 'We should have done this three days ago,' he said. Dish after dish – including the steak and the fish pie – came in over £10, to Blumenthal's intense surprise and discomfort. 'When they get these figures, they are going to get a heart attack,' he said of the Little Chef head office. However, he was under no illusion as to what was at stake: 'My reputation is going to hang on the first two weeks.'

As it was, when he told Pegler about the costings, the chief executive was less shocked than his star chef feared and was willing to see if the lower-profit-margin food brought in more customers and, therefore, ultimately, higher profits.

Blumenthal was delighted when he returned to Popham to view the now complete refit. With its clean, tiled-white floors and bright-red furniture, it looked astonishingly good, its theme influenced by classic American diners. The concept had been turned into something modern. 'It just sings vibrancy,' said Blumenthal, recalling that, when he first saw the old layout, he had thought it akin to 'an old people's home'. There was even a cheeky little detail, which he took great delight in pointing out to the crew. Throughout the project, he had been told by Pegler that what was being asked of him was blue-sky thinking, and he had asked Rogers to paint the ceiling with a blue-sky theme. Another feature was that the toilets played music when customers approached them and the smell of fresh coffee was piped into them in the hope of enticing those merely using the toilets as a stop-off point to actually stay in the restaurant and purchase some refreshments.

There were thumbs up all round from the Popham staff for the new design, and their initial concerns over what the experimental Blumenthal might do to the decor of the branch had been allayed. Branch manager Cook was delighted with the new look. 'Fuck me, this is something else,' he said, adding that the restaurant appeared to have been 'dragged kicking and screaming into the 21st century'. Cook was revising his views about Ashley, too. 'When I first met Ash, I thought, Oh my God, I can't stand you, you are just so up your own arse, I really can't be doing with you,' he admitted. 'But now my taste buds have been revitalised [by eating some mussels Ashley had cooked] and I can't wait for him to bring in a dish.'

On the evening of the launch of the new restaurant, a specially invited guest list arrived to see what Blumenthal had done. These included food critics such as Jay Rayner (who jokingly said that Little Chef is a British institution –

'mind you, so is Broadmoor'), Matthew Fort and Fay Maschler, celebrities including Anneka Rice and even designer Kevin McCloud, who said of the decor: '[I] don't like the sky, but I do quite like the soft lighting.'

Not everything went perfectly on the night. The guests who had been invited to arrive at different times all descended on Popham at once. Jason spilled chips in front of Blumenthal's wife Zanna, and Rayner was served cold macaroni cheese. However, the evening was an overall success, prompting Fay Maschler – a critic Blumenthal was especially keen to impress –to describe it as the 'restaurant opening of the year'. This praise moved Blumenthal immensely. There were kind words coming from Zanna, too, who said, 'I'm really proud of him.'

As for the man himself, he declared the experience 'quite magical' and toasted the success with his team over a glass of champagne.

After the subsequent two-week trial of Blumenthal's menu was complete, he drove to Sheffield for a meeting with Pegler. On the agenda was the question of whether his menu would be rolled out nationally. 'This is the single most important day in this whole project,' said Blumenthal, 'this is D Day.' The feeling was shared by those among the staff he'd worked with at Little Chef.

Once in the meeting, Blumenthal quickly learned that the branch had made a 'moderate loss' in the two weeks. However, Pegler was not distracted by this and said he planned to continue with the menu and roll it out more widely. Blumenthal was pleased, but was concerned that

Little Chef would keep his dishes, but replace the ingredients with cheaper versions. 'If there is any change, I will consult you first,' said Pegler. 'If you say "No", then we won't do it.'

The pair shook hands and Blumenthal later said of the chief executive, 'I am surprised, I misjudged him a bit.'

The Popham branch team were delighted to hear that the menu would be continuing. Blumenthal praised them again and said, 'This is where we step back and let you guys do it.' He concluded at the end of the series that the Little Chef project had 'been one of the hardest things I've ever tried to do'.

As for the Little Chef corporation, it had its final word on its website. 'Working with Heston has been a great experience and we are due to meet him again... to discuss the future,' ran the story. 'In the meantime, if you want to sample the new-look Little Chef for yourself, then head down to the Popham restaurant and enjoy the food, the games and the service... and believe us when we say that a trip to the loo will never be the same again.'

Some journalists were among those who did head down to the Popham restaurant. Sam Wollaston of the *Guardian* visited the branch in the wake of the show. 'The place, like the show, could have been tightened up a lot,' he wrote. 'Service was snail-porridge paced. Come on, this is a roadside cafe, people are on the way somewhere, they can't spend all day. And then the bill. Okay, so on the menu it doesn't look that expensive, we did have three courses, a couple of extras and some wine, but 50 quid! At Little Chef!

How did that happen?' He then took a positive turn, heaping praise on Blumenthal's influence on the branch. 'Anyway, moans over, it was bloody good to be honest, a thoroughly decent lunch, and much, much better than the Little Chef of old. They've done the place up, too, with smart red tables and a central communal-eating bit. We sat with a lady from Dorset who found her croissant a bit soggy but the coffee good. There were some interesting musical surprises in the loos – no room to elaborate here. And on the ceiling a lovely skyscape: white puffy clouds and seagulls.'

Liz Thomas of the *Daily Mail* also swung by. How would the favoured newspaper of Middle England find the Blumenthal-influenced Little Chef? 'The breakfast, which boasts sausages with double the meat content and award-winning black pudding, tasted healthier,' she wrote approvingly. 'The mussels were fresh and light but I can't see many being brave enough to order shellfish from a service station. The ox cheeks are great winter fare in a lovely rich sauce but it's a heavy meal and not ideal if you have another few hours of driving ahead of you. Without doubt, the best bit if you have children is the chocolate fondue. There are assorted flavours of ice cream, a thick chocolate sauce bubbling in its own pot over a candle, and a selection of extra treats to generally make a mess with.'

With the upmarket and middle-market newspapers both impressed, what would the tabloid press make of it all? Alun Palmer of the *Sunday Mirror* was sceptical. 'If you pop in to his Little Chef at Popham expecting an out-of-this-world dining experience, prepare to be disappointed,' he wrote. 'There is actually very little change to the old menu. And – as we know from Heston's moans on the TV show – the kitchen lacks the scientific equipment for experimenting that he has at his Michelin-starred restaurant The Fat Duck, in Bray.'

When the present author visited the Popham branch of Little Chef some months after the show's broadcast, it was overflowing with customers. There was a queue for tables and an air of quiet but palpable excitement in the air. The chilli con carne and Olympic breakfasts were both impressive by any standards, not least those of a motorway restaurant. The black pudding of the breakfast was particularly tasty and drew compliments from several tables. Despite how busy the restaurant was, the service remained attentive, fast and polite. As customers took their first mouthfuls, they would often nod appreciatively at each other.

Not everyone was impressed, though. One passing labourer interrupted his breakfast to telephone a friend. 'I'm at that Little Chef what that 'Eston Blooming done up,' he told him. 'Nah, it's rubbish; they should 'ave stuck to what they knew.' You can't please them all, 'Eston.

As for Blumenthal, he found the entire experience trying but said that he learned a great deal throughout the process. 'Like, how difficult it really is to run a restaurant like this,' he said. 'There comes a point where you have to use the "compromise" word. At The Fat Duck, that word doesn't exist. The scale is so different – it's a different world. Suddenly I'm working with two tonnes of fish batter. And dealing with big companies has been a learning experience.

I called someone back at this one supplier and they said, "Sorry. He doesn't work here." I said, "I just spoke to him 20 minutes ago!"'

It had been eye-opening for him and had brought him to the attention of yet more of the public. His place in the affections of the British people was secure: he was the boyish, scientific cook who made us all laugh when he came face to face with the world of Little Chef.

It was a productive experience for the restaurant, as was confirmed in May 2009 when it was decided that Little Chef would indeed use the Blumenthal menu nationwide. 'We are looking at a roll-out programme,' announced Pegler. 'First of all we will trial it in other parts of the country. Popham is unique. We've realised that people will travel out of London to eat there – we've made a destination of it. People are using it as a dining-out experience. My feeling at the moment is that the changes should only be minimal, and around supply issues,' he said, adding that year-on-year sales figures were up by 8 to 12 per cent.

The first series to come out of Blumenthal's relationship with Channel 4 had been a success: it was time for the next step in his televisual journey. It was on far more comfortable ground for the experimental, zany masterchef as he travelled to the place in which he is most interested... the past.

CHAPTER SEVEN

THE VIBRATOR AND THE COCKENTRICE

During one of Heston Blumenthal's first meetings with Channel 4 after he signed for the network, he was asked what sort of shows he wanted to make. 'I think I come across best on TV when I'm genuinely excited about something and I'm really fascinated with historical recipes,' he told them. He didn't just want it to have to be about recipes that were doable at home. The broadcaster took him at his word. 'I wanted it to be the kind of thing people could just relax and enjoy. So Channel 4 came back and suggested doing some historically themed programmes. We would pick four periods of history and create a feast inspired by each era.' Blumenthal was excited by this idea and happily agreed. *Blumenthal's Feasts* was born.

'It's certainly not a food-history programme,' he said, announcing the new series. 'We're not recreating feasts exactly as they were, we're giving them a contemporary twist. I learned a lot and it enabled me to try out some dishes that I'd read about over the years and wondered what it would be like to serve to people.'

The premise of the series was that the future of cooking lies in the secret recipes of the past. To this end, Channel 4 commissioned the chef to journey back in time and investigate historical and mythical culinary worlds before recreating the finest dishes from the eras (with his own twist of course) for celebrity-attended 21st-century banquets. His gastronomic quest saw him travel back to Victorian Britain, to Tudor England for the medieval era and to ancient Rome.

The series was executive produced by Pat Llewellyn, the managing director of independent production company Optomen. Optomen had form in gastronomic broadcasting, having put together BBC2's *Two Fat Ladies* and *The Naked Chef*.

The episode devoted to the food of ancient Rome was marvellously memorable for all who saw it. It is a time that excites Blumenthal for its sense of drama. 'One era I am desperate to explore because it was exciting, it was theatrical, it was extreme, was the Roman empire,' he smiled at the head of the show. 'The dishes they created were out-of-this-world – I want some of that.' He said that the Romans had 'lusty, if unusual appetites', and ate everything from flamingos to parrot tongues and jellyfish. They were also, he revealed, the first people to write their recipes down. No wonder they held such interest for Heston. His ambition here was to create not just a meal, 'but a theatrical spectacle that astounded diners' of the sort that deviant Roman emperor Caligula would have eaten in the first century BC. 'That's exactly what I try and do in my cooking.'

The celebrities arrived and there was some trepidation in the air. Humorist Danny Wallace, for instance, said, 'I am hoping nothing we are served will be dripping with blood, and I am hoping nothing on the plate will be alive.'

Broadcaster Alexander Armstrong, meanwhile, was expecting grapes to be dangled into his mouth.

It was to prove an unforgettable evening for all the guests, thanks to Blumenthal's knowledge and huge ambition. This was fertile ground for the imaginative chef as he explained to the viewers – at Roman feasts it was not unheard of for hundreds of ostrich brains to be served. So Wallace indeed had every reason to feel apprehensive. Blumenthal then added that, for the starter, 'In the spirit of Caligula – who enjoyed eating the private parts of various things, various creatures – we're actually making pork scratching... but from nipples.' It was a bizarre opener that few chefs other than Heston Blumenthal would even consider, let alone attempt: pig's nipple scratching.

He cooked the nipples – where he got them from was not revealed – until they were crisp and then mixed them up with salt, coriander and pepper. 'Animals' sexual organs symbolised wealth and power and were eaten by the elite,' he explained as he cooked.

But would his celebrity guests feel like the elite as they tucked in? 'It's a very erect nipple; it must have been cold,' said TV presenter Lisa Butcher, but that didn't stop her from eating them.

Actress Greta Scacchi was nowhere near as keen. 'Would anybody like more of my nipples?' she asked her fellow diners.

A thumbs-down from the actress there and the main course was going to be no less bizarre. 'Believe it or not, I think that calves' brains, rose petals and savoury custard can be delicious,' said Blumenthal. To which end he revealed what his next dish would be: calf's brain custard. 'I'm convinced there's a great dish in there somewhere,' he said of this astonishing concept. He then added that a sauce called garam was widespread in Roman times. 'They were wild about this stuff,' he said. 'It was used in 90 per cent of dishes, made from the guts of a still-gasping fish and fermented in the sun for three months.' With garam hard to come by in the 21st century, he tried to blend the brains with a Thai fish sauce as a substitute. ''Ave it!' he shouted excitedly, as they blended the four brains with the sauce. Sadly, the smell was revolting and made all and sundry positively gag with revulsion. 'Oh Jesus, have you smelled it?' asked a horrified Heston. 'I've unleashed a beast.' Bravely, he dipped a spoon in and tested how the foul-smelling concoction tasted. 'It tastes nowhere near as bad as it smells,' he said. All the same, he felt he had to ditch the Thai fish sauce idea and try to create his very own modern-day garam sauce.

It was time to head west to Devon, to go out on a fishing trip for mackerel. There, he got his mackerel to turn into garam. 'I'd never heard of garam before we [met] Heston. I would say it is the last thing I would like on my chips,' said

Chris Roberts, captain of the Salcombe fishing mission that caught the fish.

Blumenthal told viewers that, although garam seemed an odd, even unpleasant, ingredient, it had modern-day commonplace equivalents. Worcester sauce, for instance, used anchovies as its mainstay. However, having achieved his mackerel, he was not in the mood to let them ferment for three months. 'I'm not the world's most patient person, that's my problem,' he said, shrugging. He simmered the mixture in brine and used a vacuum pump to filter them. He created, he said, 'A delicate-but-rich broth made from shrimp shells. It's rather delicious. These Romans might not have been so bad after all.'

As the food was served to the celebrities, Blumenthal was anxious, looking on from the kitchen. 'I know brains won't be to everyone's taste,' he said. 'It all counts for nothing if people who are eating this actually don't enjoy it.'

Danny Wallace grudgingly admired Blumenthal's chutzpah in serving such a dish. 'What a clever trick Blumenthal's played on me,' he raved. 'I've never been so surprised by food.'

There was plenty more surprises to come, not least in the form of the next dish which Blumenthal hoped would be 'a show stopper' – a Trojan hog. Introducing it to the viewers, he explained that, for Romans, 'It's not just about taste and flavour, it's about what they see, they hear, they smell.' They were, after all, the people who invented dinner theatre. 'I suppose I've inherited the Roman love of food drama,' he added. The Trojan hog would be dramatic indeed: a whole roasted hog that would be slit open at the table to reveal what appeared to be intestines. However, these 'intestines' were really edible sausages that had been placed inside the hog in the kitchen.

To learn about the sausage-making craft, he travelled to Italy to visit an eccentric Italian sausage man called Pepe, who quickly confused an amused Blumenthal by putting a roll of ham to his lips and saying, 'I will play the trumpet.' Pepe might have been a character but, as he revealed later, he was aware of Blumenthal before the filming. 'I once cooked a pasta he had done when I held a "dinner show" for a group of friends who are also my customers.'

However, this was only the start of the task ahead. 'This might be one of the most difficult things I've done,' said Blumenthal. 'Sometimes I do question why I seemingly make life difficult for myself. Why do I feel the need to attempt things that might seemingly be impossible? And this is no exception. Fortunately when a dish like this gets under my skin and in my blood I've got no choice, it's almost like some magnetic force pulling me.'

The next place that magnetic force pulled him to was, of all places, a hot tub company where he hoped to find a spa big enough to cook a whole hog in. 'I want some beautiful big pots that you can cook a pig in,' said Blumenthal. It was an astonishing venture.

'Yes we were surprised at first at the request,' admitted Tony Burnett of the Canadian Spa Company, 'but, after giving it some thought and having seen some of Heston's work before, it didn't really seem weird at all.'

Burnett said that the resulting hog did not look appealing, but at least gave off some tempting odours. 'It didn't look too chipper when it came out, it hadn't changed colour and the bag was full of its juices,' he said. 'Having said that, I've seen some pretty rotten sights getting out of my spa after a few hours, so you can't really blame the poor little porker for not looking his best, eh? Sure, I'd have eaten it; there was a strange bacony kind of smell emanating from it which if I'm honest aroused my taste buds!' Blumenthal also showed an undiminished appetite for a puns: 'I made a pig's ear of that oinkment,' he quipped at one point.

On a more serious note, he defended his eccentric approach to food, denying that it was a sign of any lack of marbles. 'I do like to think I'm a relatively normal bloke, by the way,' said Blumenthal. 'I'm very inquisitive. If there wasn't a serious reason for doing this, I wouldn't be doing it.'

He put together two types of 'intestine sausages' for the Trojan hog. The small intestine looked like a white hot dog that included chick pea, ginger and carrot and the large intestine was a brownish, grey colour and had cocoa in it. He placed the 'intestines' inside the hot-tub-cooked hog, and the Trojan hog was ready to be served to his unsuspecting guests. 'They might just walk out after this,' grinned Blumenthal.

This time he accompanied the dish to the dining room, rather than watching from the kitchen.

'Why Trojan?' asked Lisa as Blumenthal brandished his knife.

'Good question,' he replied, and slit open the hog to reveal the 'intestines'. Looking at what they were about to be served, Armstrong joked, 'Thank heavens for little intestines.' And, having actually eaten it, he was every bit as impressed. 'Damn-it-to-crikey goodness,' he purred, 'that's the most delicious thing I've ever eaten.'

For the dessert, Blumenthal was aiming for an 'orgasmic finale' – an 'ejaculating cake'. 'I love the Roman sense of humour in cooking,' he said, smiling. As to where he would begin his research for the cake, it was as surprising as ever. 'Where better to start for ejaculating cakes than in the car park?' he asked.

Blumenthal and his team had an afternoon of boyish experimentation, toying with various exploding concoctions, including mints placed in cola bottles, which create a surprising – and for the team exciting – eruption. Then he and his colleagues hid, giggling with excitement, behind a car as a potent, dry-ice explosion tore a cake to pieces. It had been good fun, but he needed a steadier hand, and for that he turned to a cake expert. 'I need a spurting ejaculation, not an explosion,' he said.

The next leg of his cake research was a more tame experience. He visited Mich Turner from the Little Venice Cake Company, no stranger to odd cake requests. 'We created a cake in the shape of a sauna, complete with naked his and her figurines, for Emma Thompson,' she later revealed. 'We have also created a pantomime-themed cake with a stage, red velvet iced curtains and characters, a three-foot round, glitter-ball cake for *Strictly Come Dancing* and a two-foot-high chocolate Buddha cake.' She had never, though, been asked to put together an ejaculating cake, she added. 'Ejaculating – no! We tend to leave the explosions to the pyrotechnics – patisserie fireworks and sparklers.'

The final product was a chocolate cake with a biscuit base. Blumenthal added some popping candy to introduce a final fizz to the orgasm. Chocolate chambers were built in to direct the 'ejaculation' of syrup. He hoped it would wow his customers, but not maim them. In Roman times, dishes such as these were designed to make the diners feel aroused. However, on the night of Blumenthal's feast, they merely made them feel bawdy. 'I want it to do it again,' said Greta after her cake had shot its load. 'Give it 20 minutes,' said Wallace cheekily.

The feast was over and Blumenthal felt he had succeeded again. 'I've shocked my guests,' he said, 'but above all I've created a truly exciting, theatrical meal of a lifetime.'

The guests for his medieval feast, too, must have felt they had the meal of a lifetime. For this episode, he drew on an era when food was important for a very specific reason. With the plague attacking Europe and the population dwindling fast, chefs played a therapeutic as well as nutritional role in public life. 'They used food as an entertaining escape from the brutality of life,' he said. Therefore, the way food was prepared was frequently highly imaginative. 'There was one dish that really attracted my attention,' explained the host, 'because it was completely mad. You took some meat and literally turned it into fruit.' It was indeed mad, as was Blumenthal's interpretation of it.

He decided to use bulls' testicles to create 'plums'. 'I'm using plums to make plums,' he cackled boyishly, enjoying both the process and the play on words. 'This next bit might bring tears to your eyes,' he warned as he pierced the testicle and drained it.

He later blogged about the testicle experience. 'The blokes in the crew definitely found it hard to watch,' he said, 'even well-hardened cameramen! It's certainly not something you see in day-to-day cookery!' He added mandarins made from chicken livers, apples constructed with minced pork and Parma ham grapes. When it was served, naturally most of the chat of the celebrity diners focused on the bulls' testicles. 'Bollocks have never frightened me,' said Germaine Greer proudly as she ate the 'plums'.

'I might be the first chef to put a testicle in Germaine Greer's mouth,' boasted Blumenthal, from the safety of the kitchen.

And well might he have stayed out of the firing line, for Blumenthal was about to serve up something that was at least as risky as testicles. Lampreys were a popular eel in medieval times, so much so that a law was passed to ensure a plentiful supply of them in Britain. In the 21st century, it is a different story and Blumenthal travelled to the Baltic country of Latvia, the country of his paternal great-grandfather, to catch some of the bloodsucking eels. Once there, he sailed with an entertaining old fisherman who said, 'When I was born, I wasn't given my mother's milk, I was given lamprey.'

On reaching dry land, he cooked some up for some

curious locals – to a not entirely positive response. 'Tastes foreign,' complained one man. 'I don't like it.'

To try to make the dish more palatable for his celebrity guests, Blumenthal visited Martins Ritins, a leading Latvian chef. Ritins showed him how to make lamprey 'nerve spaghetti'. 'Taking the nerve out of the lamprey when it is very fresh is very simple,' explained Ritins. 'This needs to be done right after it has been netted. If not fresh, it breaks in small pieces and then is impossible to take out neatly. It tastes somewhere between exotic popcorn and a shrimp cracker.' However, Blumenthal eventually decided that the best way to do it was to steam and barbeque the eel before serving it with lamprey blood. 'It sounds a bit *Hammer House of Horror*,' said Ritins later, 'but you have to remember that blood is a natural flavouring and thickener. Without it, traditional black pudding would just be little chunks of meat.' The dish was served on a bed of edible sand.

But his guests were not overly impressed by this course. 'I'm not fond of seeing blood run loosely around a slab of marble,' complained Craig, echoing that Hammer House conclusion reached by Ritins.

As for Blumenthal, he had found his brush with the Latvians scary enough without having to worry about his subsequent bloody dish. 'All these guys had been fishing for lamprey all their lives and weren't too keen on outsiders coming in and cooking their national dish,' he later wrote on his blog. 'By the end of the ordeal I think we turned them around though, but for a second I was worried I wasn't going to escape alive.'

Of the celebrities' negative response to the lamprey course, he admitted his crushing disappointment. 'It was devastating because we'd put so much time and effort into the dish,' he said.

'Four and 20 blackbirds, baked in a pie,' goes the line in the well-known 'Sing a Song of Sixpence' nursery rhyme. Little did whoever wrote it know that it would give Blumenthal ideas. The medieval cooks used to hide all manner of things in their pies, including dwarves and frogs, but it was the concept of the blackbirds that captured Blumenthal's imagination as he prepared the medieval feast. 'It's so unbelievable, I have to do it,' he smiled.

He made a huge pie (using 40 kilos of lard and 80 kilos of flour and rolling out the dough with a bulldozer) and searched for a potter to find an oven large enough to bake the resultant pie in. As blackbirds are a protected species, Blumenthal had to use pigeons instead. It was pigeon meat that formed the basis of the pie itself and, having taken the pies to a football match where he received favourable feedback, he was ready to serve them to his celebrity guests. 'I've never cooked a dish and served it with a live animal inside,' he said. 'Ever since I read this recipe I wanted to know what the look on the diners' faces would be.'

The looks on their faces were decidedly scared as the pigeons emerged and flapped around wildly. 'A bird just shat on my head,' said Andi.

Their feathered friends eventually calmed down and it was time to taste the pie. It received a thumbs-up all round.

For dessert he made chocolate cutlery. 'I'm filling my knives with a ginger and chocolate ganache,' he laughed. 'It doesn't matter how old we are, we still like to have fun.' He also served his guests edible napkins, white chocolate candles filled with caramel and pork pie made from ice cream. He introduced these to his unsuspecting diners via a quick trick. They were asked to take a two-minute break. When they returned, their original tableware had been replaced by edible versions. 'Ladies and gentleman,' said the maitre d', 'your dessert is in front of you.'

There was mass confusion from the guests at first. 'Are we meant to eat the cutlery?' wondered Greer.

They then realised what had happened and began to tuck into the edible cutlery and crockery with enthusiasm.

Blumenthal was delighted by their response. 'They've made a right royal medieval mess,' he smiled. 'I think I've pushed it as far as I could.' It had been an imaginative experience for the guests, not least the edible tableware course. 'It was hilarious because none of the guests worked out what was going on straight away,' he said. 'Even when they were told that everything was edible, it took them a while to suss out that included the cutlery and the candles. We had to coordinate the service very effectively to stop any chocolate melting. I think they were definitely amazed by it all – and it's that childlike amazement combined with great food that sums up what I'm trying to achieve in all these feasts.'

Victorian values might get a bad press in these modern times, but the food of that era is a different matter. Not least for Blumenthal – who is fascinated by it. At the start of his Victorian feast, he announced, 'I want to create meals that are a delicious spectacle, where every bite is a delight to the senses.' This was an era he had a special, literary, connection with. 'I loved it because I love *Alice in Wonderland* – I think it's a fantastic, surreal story, I love the dark bits to it. The dark undertone to it and the way that Alice tries to apply a logical thought process to completely bizarre situations. There's an adult-kid thing in the story and the way that we never lose our inner child and the idea that through food we can actually create.'

To kick it off, he turned to a fictional beverage – the Drink Me drink from the novel, its ingredients being toffee, hot buttered toast, cherry pie, custard, pineapple and turkey. Quite a combination of flavours there, even for Blumenthal. 'It's a magical drink that never existed – that's like a red rag to a bull,' he smiled. To make it, he infused each of the ingredients in a huge container of milk, and it fascinated his guests.

One of the poshest foods of Victorian times was turtle, shipped in at great expense from the Caribbean. Blumenthal visited America to get his hands on some. Going fishing for turtles, he was in cautious mood, with good reason. 'They'll take your finger and won't let go,' he said. 'You have to put a wire up their nose to make them let go.'

He spent a couple of hours on the resultant dish – far less than the 48 hours that Victorians commonly spent putting turtle recipes together – but was less than satisfied with the outcome. 'It might be a challenge too far to make this work,' he mused. He decided instead to try 'mock turtle soup', which is actually made from cow's head, with added beef stock, ham, lemon and sherry. A good start, thought Blumenthal, but – surprise, surprise – he wanted to take it on another stage. 'It's not Lewis Carroll, is it? I need to take this and make it properly Victorian – that means trippy.' To make this work, he created an edible watch, in homage to the antics of the Mad Hatter when he dipped his watch into a tea cup. He took some stock and put it through a complicated process of freezing, filtering and centrifuge. He then covered it in gold leaf. The celebrities were impressed, and the chef will no doubt have been proud when he heard TV news reporter Rageh Omar say, 'Blumenthal is the Mad Hatter here.'

He loved the idea of insects as food. It was a popular foodstuff among Victorians, particularly as a choice for the hard-up and, to explore the notion in more detail, Blumenthal paid a visit to insect expert George McGavin, Honorary Research Associate at the Oxford University Museum of Natural History. He passed Blumenthal a pupa and said, 'They are exactly what we need to eat.'

His host was not at all fazed by Blumenthal's plans. 'I was surprised that he had not done more cooking with insects,' said McGavin. 'We can't feed the world on beef and the fish is running out fast. Insects are going to be the future. There are more than 40 tonnes of them for every human being alive.'

The chef was not entirely convinced by the experience. All the same, it had been an educational and enjoyable visit for both men.

'[It was] great fun,' smiled McGavin. 'Heston really liked my mealworm flour bread. My kitchen has never looked so clean – I decided I would need to scrub the hob prior to filming; it took rather a long time.'

After all his research for his dish, Blumenthal settled on an edible garden that featured black olive soil, paths of gravel, fried eel and waffle cones, miniature vegetables and potato pebbles. It was an ambitious, imaginative affair but was as nothing compared to what came next: a saucy, somewhat phallic-related jelly. Kathryn Hoyle of the Sh! sex store showed Blumenthal the ropes as he sought inspiration for his risqué dessert. 'We loved meeting Heston and his team and their how-to-make-a-jelly-wobble experiments actually ended up teaching us a little more about vibrators – which after 16 years in the business is no mean feat,' she said. 'Jelly turned out to be pretty good for observing the different kinds of intensity vibrators can deliver. While we know that high, zingy vibes feel different to deep, throbby ones, actually seeing the difference – from barely discernible quiver to slow ripple – has made it easier to visualise and therefore to explain the difference to customers.'

And Blumenthal's vibrating tongue certainly raised eyebrows among his guests.

'It left a mad taste in the mouth,' wrote Tom Sutcliffe of the *Independent* in a pun that would surely have met with Blumenthal's approval. He continued, 'I doubt that Blumenthal is going to have problems filling the reservations book because… [it's] a wonderful advertisement for the kind of edible hallucinations that are his hallmark. From the very beginning, he made no bones about the fact that this was for culinary voyeurs, not would-be participants.' He said he felt digestively emotional at the conclusion of the show. 'I found, you lay back on the sofa feeling a bit bloated and ever-so-faintly nauseous,' he said. 'Great fun watching him work, though, so I suspect the appetite will have returned by next week.'

Serena Davies, writing in the *Daily Telegraph*, was also mightily impressed. 'He was entertaining and original, never annoying or patronising, and I switched off the television feeling I'd genuinely learned something outside of a bog-standard account of Victorian predilections we all knew about anyway,' she wrote.

It was a show that was received warmly north of the border too. 'Lewis Carroll would have loved the meal,' wrote Andrea Mullaney in *The Scotsman*, 'though Blumenthal surely missed a trick in the historical fact that hatters were often "mad" as a result of mercury poisoning through the process of curing felt hats. Surely he could have found a way to make a mercury mousse or something?' Mullaney concluded that: 'There's a sort of glory in his spiralling experiments,' but wondered whether celebrities were vital to the viewers' enjoyment.

It was time for the Tudors to enter the reckoning. For this episode, Blumenthal returned to what he described as an era when dining was 'extravagant, flamboyant and spectacular'. He was clearly a fan of the period and it had struck a chord with him. Explaining his mission statement for the episode – and his career in general, it could be argued – he alluded to a spirit of intrepidness. 'I think food should be fun, a delicious spectacular adventure,' he said. 'I want to create meals that people will remember for the rest of their lives.' For the feasts' series, he was looking backwards to move forwards, as he explained. 'I believe the future of cooking lies in the secrets of the past,' he said. 'I'm on a food adventure in the extreme.' He was thrilled to be recreating and investigating the Tudor era. 'This period has a particular draw for me,' he said wistfully. 'This was the first golden age of English cookery. We ruled Europe in gastronomy.' One senses that Blumenthal would like to have been there at the time. Since that era, he felt, the English had lost their position as leaders. His mission for the show was simply stated but grandiose: 'I want to recapture some of that lost greatness and make us really proud of our culinary heritage.'

The guests changed each night and among the six were television presenter and DJ Alex Zane, who on arrival said of Blumenthal, 'He's mental, Heston. He's like the mental food man.' Then came television royalty in the form of Cilla Black, the national treasure who had presented such much-loved shows as *Blind Date*. Asked how adventurous she was when it came to food, she said, 'I love me offal, I draw the line at pig's feet.'

It would prove interesting to see how she responded to some of the crazy dishes Blumenthal planned to serve Black and her fellow guests. The same could be said, only even more so, of Kelvin Mackenzie. An ever-controversial figure, Mackenzie had been editor of the *Sun* newspaper during the

1980s and his coverage of the Hillsborough football stadium disaster caused such a stir that it caused a boycott of the newspaper by many Liverpudlians. He was a man not afraid to voice his opinions and his opinions of Blumenthal's food were far from complimentary. 'The grub itself, I didn't enjoy,' he said of his visit to The Fat Duck. 'I am more of a steak-and-kidney-pie guy.'

As Blumenthal later explained, he was pleased by the extra challenge that Mackenzie's presence gave to the project. 'The programme makers wanted to invite guests who are a real cross-section to generate conversation and opinion, and you always run the risk of someone going against the grain,' he said. 'I had no idea what Kelvin was going to make of it all, but that's half the fun – especially if you manage to completely change their preconceptions through the course of the meal.'

It was to be a meal that started with an aperitif to raise the eyebrows of both the diners and the viewers at home: Butter Beer, the drink that is favoured by the wizards in the *Harry Potter* novels. Introducing it to the viewers, Blumenthal put it into historical context. 'Forget Shakespeare,' he said, 'if there's something the Tudors pioneered, it's something we enjoy doing more than anything else. It's drinking beer.'

To look more closely at the drink, he visited an ancient St Albans pub called Ye Olde Fighting Cocks. One of several pubs that claims to be the oldest in England, it is just beside the River Ver and was a perfect venue for such a historical drink to be tested. There he met real-ale expert Roger Pross.

'The recipe sounds utterly revolting,' Blumenthal said, grimacing as he added beer, egg yolks, sugar and a dash of nutmeg to a pan. Then came the key ingredient: a dish of sweet butter. The result was far from visually appetising. 'It looks more like something you'd throw up after too *many* beers,' the chef said with a frown. However, when he came to drink it, he was more impressed. 'Actually I have to say that's a lot nicer than I expected it to be,' he said. He then allowed other pub customers to test it and most of them were favourably surprised by the drink, with one describing it as 'creamy and sweet'.

At the feast, Blumenthal added a froth to the top of the drink and proudly announced that his 'Tudor curtain-raiser' was ready to be served. The response of the guests was mixed. Pop singer Sophie Ellis-Bextor was very impressed. 'I thought it was yummy,' she said. 'It was Christmassy to me.'

However, it proved a 'step too far' for Mackenzie, who was dismayed by the mixture of alcohol and sweetness.

Next up, Blumenthal planned to serve a blancmange, which he explained was considered 'a real gastronomic luxury' in the 1570s, which took advantage of the fact that the Tudors loved the taste of sweet and savoury together. While reading ancient manuscripts to research a possible main ingredient for the dish, he had discovered, he explained, that frogs were considered fish during Tudor times. An inspired, cheeky grin spread across his face and, as his eyes lit up, he said, 'How can I resist?' A blancmange frog: who else but Blumenthal would attempt such a thing?

He had to travel all the way to New York City for the

main ingredient. Until he filmed the *In Search of Perfection* series, he had never visited the Big Apple, but since that first visit he had returned many times. This time around, he went straight to Chinatown to seek out some live frogs. Some local experts showed him first where to buy such creatures and then – to the horror of some viewers – how to 'humanely dispatch' them: a swift beheading, on camera. After their summary execution, they were turned into, in Blumenthal's words, 'a froggy almond smoothie', with pomegranate and sugar added.

'Was it a culinary epiphany?' asked New York journalist Ed Schoenfeld when Blumenthal tested it.

'I certainly wouldn't say this was a life-defining moment in my career as a chef,' admitted Heston.

Asked later what he thought of the dish, Schoenfeld said, 'The euphemistic "interesting".' He added, 'It was fun to make the blancmange from fresh-pressed almond milk – unfortunately, the finished dish with the ground frog mixed in was not something that would appear on my "can't-wait-to-eat-it-again" list, though it did make the "unforgettable" list.'

To complete the course, Blumenthal made deep-fried frogs' legs to use as creamy dippers. It's like KFC, quipped one of his colleagues. 'Yes,' laughed Blumenthal, 'Kermit Fried Chicken.'

The dish was still not complete in his mind, though. He wanted to create a 'froggy environment' to serve it in. The edible habitat was constructed from a hollowed-out log with a jellied pond and water-lily bowl, topped with historic delicacies from the four corners of the world. 'This is true, over-the-top Tudor style,' he said.

Cilla Black was impressed with the dish, calling it 'delicious', but Mackenzie was still not won over. 'I prefer the plate to the food,' he sniffed.

In Tudor times, explained Blumenthal when introducing the next dish, 80 per cent of food eaten was meat. For one extravagant banquet to impress the King of France, Henry VIII spent the equivalent of £5 million on a feast which included 2,000 sheep, 1,000 chickens and a whole dolphin. As his homage to this, Blumenthal wanted to create an edible mythical monster: a cockentrice. This amazingly ambitious and downright kooky venture really got Blumenthal excited. 'Just the thought of that makes the hairs on the back of my neck stand up,' he smiled.

For this lofty project, he visited – who else – but two plastic surgeons, including Peter Arnstein. He read out the recipe for the original cockentrice to Arnstein: 'Join the fore partye of the Pigge to the hinder partye of the Capoun and then stuffe hem as thou stuffest a Pigge'.

Arnstein smiled and said, 'Just my normal Sunday procedure.'

As they worked on connecting the pig and chicken, Blumenthal played the role of the surgeon's assistant perfectly, handing over implements when requested – 'Scalpel!' Arnstein laughed and said, 'We should employ him!'

They then used wire to tie together the bones of the two animals.

Asked later whether he was tempted to ask the plastic

surgeon to give the new creature a breast enhancement, he laughed. 'Ha! The idea with the plastic surgeon was to try and replicate the original Tudor recipe. To be honest, it was freaky enough without the need for any extra appendages.'

As for Arnstein, he had enjoyed working with Blumenthal. 'Heston was enormously affable and easygoing,' he said, 'with obvious bountiful energy and many ideas. As surgeons, we generally try to put the right bits back together, although I suppose transplant surgery has a vague similarity.'

Blumenthal has always wanted an element of theatre to his food and he certainly created a spectacle when he took the cockentrice to his local kebab shop, thus fulfilling the 'roast it on a spit' directive from ye olde recipe book, which said that the creature must be cooked for an hour that way, to reach Tudor perfection. Naturally, the customers were amused to see the cockentrice, one saying that it was the sort of thing he would expect to see on sale at Ozzy Osbourne's mansion. A couple of customers even tried a sample and were impressed with the taste. Blumenthal, though, was not so sure. He wanted to create a truly spectacular Tudor dish, 'And this is not it,' he sighed. It was time to return to the drawing board.

As if combining a pig and a chicken wasn't astonishing enough, for take two Blumenthal initially tried an even zanier combination: python, crocodile, camel, kangaroo, zebra and ostrich. He quickly found that many of these meats were far too tough and dry, though. It stood to reason, really. 'There's a reason why people eat beef and pork and lamb and chicken and duck and not python,' he concluded.

He then learned that, in Tudor times, the meat would often be brought to the table with the feather or fur still on. Back came that inspired grin: 'That's given me an idea.' He turned to taxidermist Derek Frampton to weld together a fur coat that combined a goose, a lamb, a hog and a chicken. It looked, as Blumenthal correctly said, like a 'mind-blowing monster'. Inside the beast, Heston combined roast chicken, lamb, pork and turkey. The meats were held together using a special protein derived from belly of a tuna.

He was still not done. Next up he popped into the Department of Chemistry at University College London, where Dr Andre Sella showed how he could introduce pyrotechnics to the occasion. The tradition of lighting the Christmas pudding is a relic from the Tudor times when chefs would light many of their foodstuffs. Using nitric acid cotton – or 'fun cotton' as Blumenthal put it – Dr Sella showed how a truly spectacular explosion of fire could be created as the cockentrice was served. 'That's it! That's it!' screamed Blumenthal when he saw the great ball of fire shoot up.

Dr Sella said later, 'Heston is a real enthusiast and has an intuitive understanding of how food works – that it is not just about taste, but about texture and presentation; the whole range of sensory experiences. Heston came to the lab armed with some simple, but key, questions. We then tried a few things out. I think enthusiasm is an understatement – he really got into the swing of things, as did the crew. He's fun to work with.'

'More than any other dish on the menu, cockentrice sums up what the Tudors were all about,' said Blumenthal as he prepared for it to be served.

As this multi-beast with its fur covering was taken into the dining room, the guests were truly astonished. 'It looks like a swan has died bumming a bear,' joked Zane.

Then the guests were given protective goggles to wear before nitric acid cotton was lit, producing a savage explosion of fire. 'Shit a brick,' exclaimed Mackenzie. 'He's gone bloody mad! He's trying to kill us!'

The meat was then served and met with widespread approval. Black smiled and said, 'It's perfect.'

Even Mackenzie was won over: 'Bit of a thumbs-up to old Heston,' he said after finishing the course.

It had been a truly astonishing invention and, as Blumenthal later revealed, they had toyed with several other crazy concepts. 'From a purely visual point of view, I guess there are no limits,' he said of the cockentrice concept. 'We did brainstorm an idea involving a crocodile head, kangaroo body and snake tail which would have looked pretty incredible. But in the end it had to come down to taste, which is why we opted for more traditional farm animals. This was great fun, though really nerve wracking at the feast – we really didn't want to set the studio on fire! We did a few tests to work out exactly how much of the flash cotton we could safely use, but even then you never know exactly what's going to happen on the night. Definitely best avoiding this at home – we had a lot of safety precautions and experts to help us do it safely.'

For the dessert, Blumenthal was serving rice pudding – with, inevitably, a difference. He went to the Ambrosia factory – home of traditional rice pudding. His host was technical manager Debra Crome, who enjoyed meeting him. 'I am sure this has been said before but he was just like he comes across on his programmes,' she said. 'He was really down-to-earth and made everyone relax around the camera. He wanted to know all about what made Ambrosia so good and was fascinated with the technical and food chemistry side of how we manufacture rice pudding.'

His pudding was different to the one served by the company, including as it did bone marrow, egg yolk and bitter berries, packed into pig's guts and cooked. However, as Blumenthal explained, he was in part following a rich tradition. 'It's funny because bone marrow has been used in pudding for centuries, and the suet pudding that we all know and love (used in desserts and savoury dishes) contains the fat from around the veal kidney, so bone marrow is not so different from this,' he said. 'It's a really good example of how we've lost touch with our food history. The bone marrow adds an amazing richness to the dish which is hard to replicate with other ingredients. I'm not sure it would add much to your hot chocolate, but a chocolate cake on the other hand...'

Blumenthal wanted his final dish to resemble bangers and mash visually. First, he tried to cook the rice pudding in a sausage cover, or as he put it, 'basically intestines – pigs' guts'. Then he experimented with the idea of cooking it in a condom, an invention that dated from the 16th century, he explained. He made the 'mash' part of the recipe from pureed bananas and then represented peas by mashing up fresh peas and preparing them using his trusty old liquid nitrogen. 'Why do it that way?' he was later asked. Why not cut out the fussiness and just use... peas? 'Real frozen peas wouldn't have worked at all. We pureed the peas and combined them with a sweet syrup and then froze them into tiny sorbet balls using liquid nitrogen. When you stick one on your tongue it tingles and disappears into nothing in a second with a sweet taste and hint of pea. Compare that to munching through a spoonful of fibrous peas straight out of the freezer!'

When it was served to the guests, they wondered why something that appeared to be bangers and mash would come at dessert time. Food critic Jay Rayner, all too familiar with Blumenthal's *modus operandi*, was clear on one thing: 'The only thing you can be certain is that it's not bangers and mash.'

Cilla Black was once more mightily impressed with the food, saying, 'The "sausage" is fabulous!'

A smiling Blumenthal was delighted with her praise: 'I got the thumbs up from Cilla!'

However, it was the increased admiration of Mackenzie that truly made him smile. 'I don't know anything about this world, but I would say this was quite delicious,' he said. 'Heston's full of tricks and games, he's a magician,' added the former *Sun* boss.

Zane was quick to have fun with Mackenzie over his turnaround. 'Kelvin, Heston's got inside your head,' he joked.

'You came here a strong man and now you've gone food mad. Heston Blumenthal's run riot on your arse tonight.'

The chef burst out laughing listening to Zane's jokey rant.

It had been an enjoyable, successful series that secured Heston's place in the hearts of the British public even more than the Little Chef series had. A follow-up was soon booked. Channel 4 commissioning editor for features, Liam Humphreys, said, 'We are absolutely delighted with the success of *Heston's Feasts*. It was highly acclaimed by critics and a big ratings success and provided the perfect platform for Heston to demonstrate his incredible talents. The second series will be a great opportunity for Heston to further explore his fascination with long-lost recipes, fairytales and nostalgia and his extraordinary feasts are guaranteed to be bigger, better and madder.'

However, as the show had been broadcast, Blumenthal had been in the headlines for all the wrong reasons as he faced every restaurant owner's worst nightmare.

CHAPTER EIGHT

THE GREAT CULINARY INVENTOR

On 28 February 2009, The Fat Duck faced a health scare and a short-lived closure after a series of customers complained of being unwell. With Blumenthal's profile enormous thanks to his recent television shows, the media pack quickly swooped on the story. 'It's not an easy decision to close the restaurant and there will be a lot of disappointed people who have bookings, but it has to be investigated,' said a spokesman for the restaurant. 'Heston wants to look after his customers – he is fanatical about food hygiene and he is flabbergasted as to how this could have happened. The restaurant will be closed for as short a time as possible but his priority at the moment is the investigation.'

Boxing promoter Frank Warren had dined at the restaurant. He had a great time there, but soon he and the diners in his group fell ill. 'I really did enjoy the experience of it all,' he told the *Daily Mail*. 'Heston's obviously a very talented guy. I watch his programmes and I hope he gets it sorted out.'

The case was investigated by the Health Protection Agency (HPA) and a spokesman for The Fat Duck said, 'If a staff member returned to work while still carrying the virus, they did so unaware they either had it or were still contagious.' For Blumenthal, his frustration was compounded by the fact that he was, he felt, especially careful when it came to food safety. 'For the last five years we've been sending food off every month for sampling and I don't know any other restaurant in the country that does that,' he said. 'We also have a company that has been looking after all our health and safety stuff for the last five years.'

The restaurant reopened on 12 March, nearly two weeks after its closure, during which time the entire premises had had a thorough cleansing. Among the first customers to return was 29-year-old George Flo. 'We booked our meal in January out of curiosity really and it has such a good reputation. It's pure coincidence that it reopened today and we did not think about cancelling. If anything, I would imagine it would be a bit more clinical today.'

The Fat Duck reported being 'delighted the Health Protection Agency and the local environmental health office have given us the all-clear to open the restaurant. We are overjoyed to be able to get back to business as normal.' Blumenthal admitted that he did at times fear the worst – permanent closure – during the traumatic episode. 'I wouldn't be human if it didn't go through my head,' he said. 'You obviously think of all the possibilities and just how bad it can be. Even when we reopened the restaurant, you worry what the response is going to be. Luckily it was fantastic, but it was a hugely worrying period. The hardest part was that, while we were dealing with the problem, our development work was put on hold. Now we are back on track.'

Of course, as we have seen, food safety has always been a paramount consideration of Heston. In his books *In Search of Perfection* and *Further Adventures in Search of Perfection*, he devotes detailed sections of the appendix to food safety. As well as more obvious tips, he advises readers that the shell of a chicken's egg often carries a great deal of bacteria and should be treated as if they are raw meat. Referring to the scare stories over outbreaks of salmonella, E coli and botulism, he writes, 'It often seems as though there's a new food scare story every week. The scare stories show that it's absolutely vital to establish a proper and effective hygiene routine in your kitchen.' This is advice he has always followed.

With The Fat Duck scare saga resolved, Heston was in the headlines for more positive reasons when he became yet more of a guru by fronting up the search for a brand-new kitchen gadget. The dishwasher tablet firm Finish and kitchenware company Lakeland launched the search for a new item of kitchenware, and the winner stands a chance of seeing their product stocked in stores across the country. A kitchen-based project involving invention and innovation, this was an initiative right up Heston's street. At the launch of the search, he said, 'The British have always been in the vanguard of great innovation and great design and kitchen innovation is no exception – I'm delighted to be at the forefront of this new challenge to find the next generation of culinary innovators.' He added, 'Great innovation is born from inspiration and from an understanding of tradition and classic innovations of the past. The entries that will stand out for me will be the ideas that bring this to life and that translate a brilliant idea from the past into something new for the kitchens and cooks of the future.'

This talk of the chefs of tomorrow shows that Blumenthal is comfortable with the idea of becoming a mentor for future cooks. 'If I could get kids to be open-minded about food and enjoy the pleasures and use that to build confidence, it would be brilliant,' he said. To which end, he would bring joy to the kitchen as the very first ingredient. 'I want to make it fun and show how much enjoyment you can get from cooking and eating. It can bring so much; it's creative, teaches technical skills and brings in all the senses and how they work and you get something delicious to eat at the end.'

Here we returned to the Heston of his childhood, dreaming of being an inventor who creates a spaceship that could go anywhere in the universe – even as far as Ireland. Having invented so much in his kitchen, he was encouraging others to follow suit. Heston had proven to be an inspiration to many – not one to gain his reputation through shouting and cursing, believing that once a chef does that then they have lost something, he is instead famous for what the competition represented: innovation.

And this was not the only public-search competition that Blumenthal was involved in at this time. He signed up to present an award at the *Which?* awards in 2009.

However, a more high-profile competition he was involved in came with quite a crunch. He spent much of the first half of 2008 working with Walkers Crisps in a venture that the company described as 'big and new and exciting'. As news seeped out about this link-up, speculation grew that Blumenthal was set to replace football legend Gary Lineker as the new face of Walkers. This was swiftly denied by both parties, and all was revealed in July when the Do Us A Flavour campaign was launched. The public were asked to submit their own suggestions for new flavours for the range. Over a million votes were received and a final six were named, each of whom won £10,000. The shortlist was then put to the public vote: Cajun Squirrel; Fish and Chips; Chilli and Chocolate; Crispy Duck and Hoisin; Builder's Breakfast and Onion Bhaji. These were surprising choices for crisps, but then there is a history of peculiar crisps tastes in the UK.

In 1981, a Welsh landlord called Phillip Lewis created Hedgehog flavour crisps. 'Savour all the flavour of traditional country fare cooked the old-fashioned way without harming a single spike of a real hedgehog,' read the text on the back of the packet.

But which of the six flavours in the Walkers search would be most savoured by the Great British public? The winner stood to receive £50,000 and one per cent of all sales of the flavour, so the stakes were high.

The search was concluded in May 2009 with the Builder's Breakfast, suggested by Emma Rushin from Derbyshire, the winning flavour. More than a million people had voted for their favourite, with 232,336 of those votes going to Rushin's flavour. Onion Bhaji came second, then Fish and Chips, Crispy Duck and Hoisin, Cajun Squirrel and Chilli and Chocolate rounded it off. Blumenthal handed Rushin the £50,000 winner's cheque and said, 'The builder's breakfast is a national institution.'

Emma was gleeful and smiled: 'I'm so proud.'

Blumenthal had enjoyed the process and approved of the six finalists' choices. 'The winner may be quite traditional,' he said, 'but with the other finalists, it just goes to show how tastes are evolving and the public are getting more adventurous. If you had offered people that flavour five years ago, they would have said, "Yuk, disgusting!" This competition gave me the opportunity to work with Walkers in the development of the flavours. Chefs can learn a lot from the expertise of food companies who are leaders in their field.'

He went on to say, 'I think chefs can learn a lot from the technical side of companies like Walkers, but sometimes what will happen is companies will say, "We want to work with you so we want all your ideas, but actually you have to sign these papers and can't use anything you've learned from this." You think, What is the motivation for doing it? So, if I'm not allowed to take any of that inspiration and take it back to my cooking, then I'm not interested in [working with them].'

As is so often the case when he discusses food, Blumenthal looked to the past when considering the potato crisp. 'I kind of grew up with crisps,' he said. 'I can remember my old man buying me my first half of shandy with a bag of crisps.' Asked how old he was at the time, he joked, 'I was only three!' Blumenthal also put this in context. 'I am really keen about trying new things and it is an exciting time for food in Britain because people are more willing to try new things than ever before. I always encourage people to be more experimental. I love prawn cocktail because of the nostalgic memories it brings back for me. We can get a bit too highbrow about the things we cook.' (And not a posh prawn cocktail either. He has separately said, 'I cannot resist a cheap, supermarket prawn cocktail, made with mushy frozen prawns and an overly sweet marie rose sauce. If I open the fridge door and see one of those, my shoulders fall, because I know I'm not going to be able to stop my hand reaching for it. It's the same with pork pies. I cannot resist a pork pie.')

TV presenter Fearne Cotton, also at the launch, said, 'It's wonderful to see the level of support people gave all of the six flavours, especially Builder's Breakfast! From sweet to sour, traditional to modern, the flavours provided such a big variety to choose from, it was never going to be easy. Congratulations to Emma Rushin!'

Blumenthal wrapped up affairs by saying, 'Our taste buds are changing and developing as new flavours and foods become readily available. Everyone has their favourite flavours but lately people are becoming keen to experiment and try new foods.'

Heston was soon rumoured to be planning to try not just new foods, but also new pastures. In April 2009, the gossip of the culinary world was abuzz with speculation that he was about to launch a new restaurant at London's Mandarin Oriental Hyde Park. It is one of the capital's most luxurious hotels, designed with elegance and attention to detail, and located in Knightsbridge with fine views over Hyde Park from the 173 rooms and 25 fine suites. The existing dining rooms there include Foliage, 'a sleek Michelin-starred' establishment according to the *Sunday Telegraph*, and The Park, which boasts that it serves 'stunning food'. Blumenthal, with his stars and stunning food, would fit in perfectly among all this and his signature for the hotel would be an enormous coup for the establishment.

He had been insistent just months earlier in an interview with the Caterer Search website that his heart and attention remained in Bray. 'I'm never going to do another one of these; it would just undermine what we're doing in Bray. I'm not saying that I'm not going to open other restaurants, but there's a lot I still want to do here,' he said. He was asked by the prescient interviewer whether he might one day open an outlet in a hotel. 'There are lots of things that I am talking about, but there's nothing definite,' was his enigmatic response. There had clearly been lots of talking going on behind the scenes, because, as far back as 2007, he had hinted he was close to a deal for a London venue. 'We're in serious discussions but it's not a done deal yet,' he told the Bloomberg website. 'It's with a site in London, a very good site in London, but I haven't signed anything.

Fingers crossed, I'm hoping we might get something one way or the other in the next months – decided. I mean, agreed on. It certainly won't be happening for, I'd say, a couple of years.'

Chris Staines, head chef at Foliage resigned, prompting increased speculation in the trade press. A spokeswoman for Mandarin Oriental Hyde Park confirmed the news and added he was leaving 'to pursue a new opportunity'. 'A replacement for Chris has been identified and an announcement will be made in due course,' she said. 'We have enjoyed an excellent working relationship with Chris over the past seven years, during which time he has been instrumental in raising the profile of Foliage as one of London's finest Michelin-starred restaurants. We wish him every success with his new venture.'

In late May, Blumenthal made a partial acknowledgement that there was substance to the stories of who was going to take over when he said that he did indeed have a venture planned in London. 'It won't be a Fat Duck but it will have a strong element of British history. I haven't signed anything yet, [but] we have been talking to the Mandarin Oriental and two or three other people for two years.'

Meanwhile, Blumenthal's tireless fascination with yet more imaginative food and science experiments continues unabated. Among other projects he was involved with in the first half of 2009 was research into the relationship between words and food. He handed his human guinea pigs two plates of food, and asked them to describe each in sounds. Reportedly, they described brie as 'very maluma' and cranberries as 'very takete'. There is no sign of him giving up his boyish, geeky enthusiasm.

He also continues to have his excellence recognised by his industry. In April 2009, El Bulli was declared the number-one restaurant in the annual guide *S Pellegrino World's 50 Best Restaurants 2009* which followed a poll of more than 800 chefs, critics and industry insiders for *Restaurant* magazine. Blumenthal's Fat Duck came second and when El Bulli's head chef Ferran Adrià accepted the award he gave the runner-up due praise. 'I dedicate this prize to Heston Blumenthal. He has shown me what honesty means in this business... This is for you,' Adrià said.

Despite his prestige in the gastronomic industry, Blumenthal is always anxious to remind the world that he is a down-to-earth guy and certainly not a food snob. 'People think that because I'm a Michelin-starred chef that I only eat lobster and caviar,' he told the *Sun* newspaper. 'Of course, that's not the case.' He then once more spoke with childlike wonder of his past, from which he took so much of the inspiration for his work. 'There's something you can't beat about the taste of your favourite childhood foods,' he said. 'I grew up in the 70s, when the only type of pasta you could get in the UK was spaghetti in a blue packet. When you went out for a family meal, it was usually served in a basket down the pub. And, of course, there was prawn cocktail with shredded lettuce in a cocktail glass. I still love shredded lettuce.'

Speaking of special, Blumenthal had a very royal visitor to The Fat Duck in 2009. Prince Philip popped into the restaurant from nearby Windsor for a bite to eat and, some days later, Blumenthal received an interesting phone call from the man himself. 'We were amazed,' said Blumenthal. 'He called the restaurant and asked us to send over the original recipe for my fish and chips so he could make it himself. He said he had watched my programme on the BBC, *Fish and Chips: In Search of Perfection*, and said he was a big fan.'

Having received his OBE from the Queen, Blumenthal had now received an honour of a different sort from her husband: a request for cooking advice. It seems certain that he will have enjoyed both.

This had not been Blumenthal's first encounter with royalty: he once prepared a liquid nitrogen-made dish in front of the royal couple. 'I think she might have been a bit nervous – I was stirring quite vigorously and some splashed over the bowl,' recalled Blumenthal. 'But she seemed to be really genuinely interested. And Prince Philip got completely stuck in. It was quite funny. He'd enjoyed my Christmas special and actually said, "This is really quite tame for you, isn't it?"'

Blumenthal took the point but is also anxious to guard against his techniques becoming unnecessarily complicated, as he is concerned about the effect this might have on the next generation of chefs. And, of course, he is keen to not lose sight of the key purpose of cooking food. 'There's been a big growth in gastronomical congresses where chefs do demonstrations,' he said. 'These combine some of the biggest names in world cooking with young, up-and-coming chefs. Younger chefs get invited to do a demo and it's a really big honour. They'll think, I can't just roast some meat and cook a few potatoes. I have to do something more creative. I think the risk is that chefs would much rather show an audience something that spins around, puffs up and then disappears, because everyone goes, "Wow that's incredible!" But that has a danger of overtaking the good old-fashioned "does it taste delicious?" approach.'

As customers need to book months in advance for a seat at Blumenthal's restaurant, it is quite clear that his food continues to taste delicious. He has become one of Britain's most-loved master chefs and a national treasure. His enthusiasm and eccentricity have struck a chord with the British public who have taken him to their hearts. There were no signs at all of his ambition and sense of adventure diminishing. His popularity soared, as he is a chef that combines both the Midas touch and the common touch. He has spent his life in search of perfection, and the rest of us get to enjoy the ride.

CHAPTER NINE

BACK TO THE FUTURE

Many men, as they cross the threshold into middle age, lose much of their reserves of energy and ambition. Blumenthal could certainly be forgiven for doing just that on reaching his mid-forties. After all, he has already richly proved himself and now enjoys the benefits and responsibilities of fame and fortune. He has bought a big house in Buckinghamshire which has, he says, 'an equally large mortgage'. So, in his case, there are an abundance of reasons for him to settle in to a comfortable, predictable life, and to eschew any nagging temptations to take any risks. However, we have seen enough of his nature by now to know that this big kid was not about to do anything of the sort.

No, in recent years he has been as bright and busy as ever. In the spring of 2010, he added a new venue to his list of Bray-based businesses. The Crown, which sits grandly across the High Street from The Fat Duck, is a delightful

16th-century inn with low-beamed ceilings and open fires; an evocative and atmospheric building, inside and out. It has enjoyed some well-known visitors in its life: local legend has it that Charles II would pop-in for a drink when visiting his mistress Nell Gwynn at Holyport. Sometimes, well-to-do visitors to Bray have stopped there for a drink before or after sampling the tasting menu at The Fat Duck. One celebrity visitor to Bray – the television personality Ulrika Jonsson – described it as being 'like the kind of pubs I would visit when I first came to England where there's a lovely community atmosphere.'

It seemed Blumenthal may have bought the building without too much planning. Even as he officially announced his acquisition, he remained open-minded as to how he would develop his new bricks-and-mortar toy. He was also mindful of the impact that his growing presence in Bray – he now owned three venues in the area – was having on the small village and its 9,000-odd residents. 'We've kept the bar at The Hinds Head but the place has become a bit of a culinary destination, so that The Crown has become the local,' he said. 'I might do a steak bar, but good meat is so expensive, I don't know if the prices would be right. I just haven't made up my mind what to do yet, though I'm not going to turn it into Bray's first lap-dancing bar or anything like that. I just want it to be the local pub.'

The residents of Bray breathed a sigh of relief. Well, most of them anyway.

In due course, a spokesperson announced there would be some changes to the venue, describing them as 'subtle but necessary improvements to the decor and furnishings, to bring it up-to-date and to provide the most comfortable setting for our guests'.

In time, the menu took shape, too. Although Blumenthal insisted that he did not wish to stray far from traditional pub grub, The Crown does offer slightly more flamboyant options than your average British boozer. Among the dishes on offer have been a soup of vanilla cream, blueberries, mandarin and thyme; Soft-boiled hens egg, ham and cheese toastie; Trug of baby vegetables, bagna càuda; Brixham mussels, white wine, garlic, parsley & fries; and Roast Loch Duart salmon, with crushed Jersey royals. This is all wonderfully Hestonseque: delicate twists on old favourites, with childlike comfort-food staples making the occasional appearance.

Meanwhile, the other arms of his empire continued to flex their muscles. Towards the end of the year, Blumenthal was given a foretaste of a trend that risks becoming a staple part of his Christmas menu. During the festive period of 2010, sections of his new food range in the Waitrose supermarket chain attracted huge orders from people who had no intention of eating them. Rather, they were buying his popular goods in bulk to sell at inflated prices on the Internet. 'That was mad,' he said, looking back, adding that he understood why the media reports of the process led to some regular customers joining in with the profiteering. 'Once they hit a thousand quid, a lot of people thought, "Stuff that, I'm sticking mine on eBay",' he said. This is a very hard process to police.

All of this meant that many people who had hoped to have one of Heston's Christmas pies were disappointed; in fact, he nearly missed out himself. 'I did have one on Christmas Day, but only by chance,' he said. 'I forgot to bloody get one, I was skiing in Italy. But a mate brought one, so we took it up to this mountain restaurant where they cooked it.' As he continued telling the story, he revealed that a spontaneous twist was added to the delicacy.

'Then my mate drizzled on cream and chocolate sauce. I thought, "What are you doing putting chocolate on a Christmas pudding?" But it was absolutely fantastic... so much so that I've done a recipe for it this year.' It was an interesting moment for Heston, one in which his traditional role was reversed. Instead of being the intrepid culinary experimenter, he momentarily became the sceptical onlooker. For a moment, he saw the sort of work he does through our eyes. 'It's weird, how we get so conditioned to eating things in a particular way – that if someone does something different, you think it's strange,' he said, adding, 'But I suppose of all people I should know that!'

As Blumenthal enjoyed the slopes of Italy, he reflected on a successful year. It was one in which both the man himself and his work were recognised by several prestigious authorities and award-givers. He was named *GQ* Chef of the Year at its prestigious 'Man of the Year' awards. Other gongs and honours he received during the year included The Fat Duck being named as the Third Best Restaurant in the World in the San Pellegrino World's 50 Best Restaurant Awards and the Trophy Gourmand of

Austria, while his *Feasts* series won a BAFTA nomination in the features category.

Forever restless, Heston enjoyed the glories of these honours but was already looking ahead to 2011, a year that would begin with him launching a new restaurant in London. That should have been the most notable event in the year to come – as it turned out it was just one moment in a hugely eventful 12 months. For indeed, while it would be an exaggeration to describe 2011 as an example of the fabled *annus horribilis* for him, it was certainly a year in which Blumenthal was often to be reminded that there is a price to fame and success. The press swooped and showered him with condemnation as his marriage came to an end, touts targeted his Christmas range at Waitrose again, and the controversy over the norovirus outbreak at The Fat Duck rumbled on.

Let us be clear, though: among the negatives there were plenty of positives. The triumph of the year for Blumenthal was the successful launch of his Knightsbridge restaurant, Dinner. While the heart of Heston's operation remains in Bray, he had long dreamt of also opening a restaurant in London, having lived in the capital for the first nine years of his life. Hyde Park – which Dinner overlooks – is one of his favourite parts of the city, and he was keen to do justice to the fine surroundings by creating a striking interior. He succeeded. For instance, in the dining room there are floor-to-ceiling glass walls, which mean people can see the kitchen's pulley system as they eat. There is a prized Chef's Table, available for up to six people; it includes exclusive access to the kitchen and team of chefs. The walls are ivory-painted and one of the bar's walls features the text of recipes from the 16th century. They disappear and reappear as if by magic, depending on the movement of light.

The historical recipes were highly relevant: for the Dinner menu, Blumenthal had scoured archive recipes to inspire parts of the menu. For instance, his Beef Royal dish was inspired by a recipe from *Royal Cookery* by Patrick Lamb, published as far back as 1710. He obsessively tested different temperatures at which to cook the dish, altering them by one degree until finally settling for a temperature of 56°C. 'There is an obsessive attention to detail,' he admitted. 'It sounds anal but one or two degrees really does make a difference.' That he had taken such microscopic and painstaking care came as no surprise to anyone.

The historical theme of many of Dinner's dishes originated from a chance meeting between Blumenthal and two food historians from Hampton Court Palace in 2003. One of the historians, Marc Meltonville, explained how they met and how their rapport grew: 'The palace team met Heston about five or six years ago. Myself and my colleague met him at a food conference in Oxford. We were pushed together in one corner and we were all having funny history ideas and getting on really well. He was very interested.' Blumenthal stayed in touch with the historians and scoured their records. 'I went up to Hampton Court and saw this wealth of stuff – recipes and other archives – and realised that, a couple of hundred years ago, we had a cuisine that was as good as anywhere else in Europe,' he told one interviewer.

In delving so far into Britain's past for inspiration, Blumenthal felt he had created something rare. While commercially this works for him, part of him wishes others would do the same. 'The historic British thing is something which is quite a unique concept – it shouldn't be, because it's celebrating what we've done in the past in cooking,' he said, adding, 'I suppose a mixture of planning and a big chunk of luck has put this restaurant in a spot that nothing else quite occupies, and I can't quite define it yet.'

Blumenthal went on to outline the effective working contrast between himself and head chef Ashley Palmer-Watts, who has since been promoted to Executive Head Chef for The Fat Duck Group. 'I'm the big kid who thinks everything is possible and he's more glass-half-empty – he'll look at practical things like how much fridge space we have got and how many covers we want to do,' he said. This culinary ying and yang continues to work for many palates.

His first restaurant in London has been a success thus far. It was named the Best Newcomer in the respected *Zagat* restaurant guide. As the guide's chief executive noted, the successful launch of Dinner gave hope to all that fine-dining was not a thing of the past, despite the economic downturn. 'You don't go to the big name restaurants unless you have a fair amount of money in your pocket,' he said. *Tatler* named Dinner its restaurant of the year for 2011 and it won the BMW Square Meal Award for Best New Restaurant. It has since also been rewarded its first, precious Michelin star.

Also in 2011, the book *Heston Blumenthal at Home* came out. Published by Bloomsbury, it is a weighty tome, and with a RRP of £30 is hardly an impulse purchase. What the book promised to bring to readers made that a price worth paying – for many of his admirers anyway. 'Until now, home cooking has remained stubbornly out of touch with technological development but Heston Blumenthal, champion of the scientific kitchen, is set to change all that with his radical new book,' read the publicity blurb. 'With meticulous precision, he explains what the most effective techniques are and why they work.' The opportunity to take his gastronomic alchemy techniques into the home was tantalising. '*Heston Blumenthal at Home* will change the way you think about cooking for ever – prepare for a culinary revolution!' concluded the publicity. Recipes were extracted and trailed in the *Guardian* newspaper, allowing more interest to be built up in time for publication.

The critics were divided. The *Evening Standard*'s Melanie McDonagh wrote: 'The book would work best for men a bit like the author: obsessive, prepared to take enormous pains and interested in process. Often he sets out to solve problems that don't exist.' Writing in the *Belfast Telegraph*, Lisa Markwell made a reasonable observation about the book, using the second 'h' word of its title to make a salient point. 'I think it's fair to say that Heston's home isn't like yours and mine,' she wrote. 'This is a stunningly beautiful, ingenious and knowledgeable book, but I wouldn't turn to it on a Thursday night for supper ideas. One for the coffee table rather than the kitchen counter.' The *Independent*'s Christopher Hirst also feared that the book was more applicable for use in The Fat Duck's kitchen, rather than those of his newspaper's readers. However, he praised Heston's 'combination of playfulness and ardent didacticism'. The *Guardian* was convinced that for the most part *Heston Blumenthal at Home* covered terrain accessible enough for the average domestic kitchen-dweller, praising the book as a 'splicing of molecular gastronomy with standard-issue domestic science, using more-or-less average kitchen kit (aside from an occasional detour via dry ice and sous-vide).'

It was in the second half of the year that Heston suffered press coverage of a far less savoury nature. In August 2011, he announced he had split from his wife Zanna after 20 years of marriage. It was simultaneously revealed that he had begun dating a glamorous American cookery author called Suzanne Pirret. As well as writing a book called *The Pleasure Is All Mine: Selfish Food for Modern Life*, his new partner had worked as an actress and as a pastry chef at Jamie Oliver's restaurant Fifteen. Pirret, who was described as a 'goddess', has posed naked in glamorous photographs. She once described food and sex as, 'Two of my favourite things, and the most powerful of all human drives,' adding, 'Best one after the other in either order, I'm not picky.' She is fond of conflating consumption and coition in a tantalising style, for example: 'When I smell an avocado I don't immediately become aroused.'

Blumenthal's new partner has been described as a 'minx from Manhattan' and a 'sauce box'. She hails from a wealthy American family. For her love of cookery she credits her late father, a company treasurer, who died unexpectedly in 1997. She left the grand family home in New Jersey to live in London. She initially crossed the Atlantic, she said, 'for love that didn't work out'. The media delighted in publishing rather raunchy images of Pirret while reporting the Blumenthals' break-up. It made for a difficult time for Blumenthal and his wife, as well as their three teenage children. A spokesman for the Blumenthals confirmed the split with an official statement: 'Over the course of their marriage, they have built an extremely successful business, but one which has unfortunately taken its toll on their relationship,' it said. 'They remain good friends and devoted parents of their three children who are their main focus.'

It is uncomfortable to recall at this stage the moving words Blumenthal used just four years previously to describe his wife. 'Zanna is the reason for my success because she has supported me every step of the way,' he had said. 'She's sacrificed so much and has never complained.' And her words about him: 'It sounds corny, but I knew from the outset that I'd found my soul mate. There was a deep connection between us and even though we were just teenagers, we knew we had found something special.' Now, two decades on, the relationship was over.

Blumenthal is not the first celebrity chef to experience marriage problems. Marco Pierre White has been married three times; one of his marriages lasted just 15 weeks. Rick Stein was 64 when he married his wife, then 21. They split after she discovered he was having an affair. All four of the late Keith Floyd's marriages ended in divorce, Tom Aikens and Gordon Ramsay have also encountered tumultuous relationships. As the *Daily Mail*'s controversial columnist Jan Moir wrote: 'Oh Heston Blumenthal, not you, too?' Moir laid into Blumenthal with trademark ferocity, describing him as 'another philandering *cliché*, like so many of his half-baked peers.'

Here, we see again the allure and power of celebrity chefs in the 21st century. Many of the famous cooks with such colourful private lives are not exactly stunners when it comes to looks. However, there is something about them that beautiful women find alluring. Chefs are now, to their delight, attracting groupies in the same way rock stars and footballers do. Rick Stein's ex-wife Jill has seen this in action. 'Those PR girls and hangers-on, you see them buzzing around the chefs all the time,' she once said. 'And most of those famous chefs, they are onto their second marriages or they have got mistresses or girlfriends on the side. They all do it.'

Blumenthal moved-out of the family home as his wife and children came to terms with the split. He and Pirret were pictured after a dinner date at the exclusive sushi restaurant Zuma, in Knightsbridge. She sported a splash of bright red lipstick, attracting plenty of attention. In November, Heston and Pirret made their first high-profile public outing. They attended a Halloween party at the home of TV presenter Jonathan Ross. They had both dressed for the theme: Blumenthal sported fake blood, vampire teeth and red contact lenses alongside his sharp black suit, while Pirret wore a low-cut emerald gown with ghoulish contact lenses and fangs.

The break-up of this marriage was not the only uncomfortable story for Heston in the second-half of 2011. In December, he learned again how success can come with a price. His food products were the stars of the Waitrose Christmas range – and as such were targeted by profiteering opportunist touts. As had been seen during the 2010 festive period, as soon as his popular orange-filled Christmas puddings went on sale at Waitrose stores and the online business that sells its goods, Ocado, touts swooped to buy as many of the £13.99 puddings as they could get their hands on. They then sold them on eBay at huge mark-ups – sometimes for as much as £250 at time. They were indeed popular – so much so that some touts were said to be offering a 'tip-off fee' to be given a heads-up on which branches were going to stock them next. As supermarket staff smelt a rat they told staff to avoid selling them in suspicious bulk. In response, the touts developed new ways of obtaining plentiful supplies of the puddings. One tout in east London told staff at a local branch that he needed to buy 50 of the puddings for a daughter's wedding. Her 'big day' would be ruined, he told them, if he was unable to buy such a quantity. Having successfully acquired them, he sold them on eBay for £99.99 a shot; he must have chuckled all the way to the bank.

Meanwhile, legitimate shoppers were leaving stores disappointed at having been unable to acquire a pudding. On the face of it, this was a disastrous trend for both Blumenthal and the Waitrose chain. A supermarket spokesman did his best to assure disappointed shoppers that there would be more Heston puddings on sale soon. 'We've done everything we can to make them available but they fly off the shelf as they're a very popular product,' she said. However, both supermarket and chef will have been aware that the story had an enormously beneficial dimension to it in terms of public relations. As national newspapers printed stories about the issue, millions of new readers were becoming interested in the idea of trying Heston's products.

Waitrose was benefiting in general from its association with his range. For the busy Christmas 2011 period it had Hidden Orange Christmas Pudding, Black Forest Buche and a new Popping Candy Tart all on sale courtesy of the master chef. While many high street chiefs bemoaned slow sales, Waitrose was bucking the trend thanks to his Christmas range. 'We have had a phenomenal response to the Heston puddings – we have upped orders by nearly 10 times this year, and in total we will have sold hundreds of thousands of puddings this Christmas,' said a spokesperson. 'We sold a fraction of this last year.' They also hired Blumenthal to pen regular contributions to the Waitrose publications, which were snapped-up by impulsive customers as they queued at the checkouts. So, the relationship between the supermarket and chef was overall a positive one, and even the eBay headlines had a positive dimension for both parties.

A news story with no immediately conceivable positive spin broke around the same time. Experts at the Health Protection Agency (HPA) who had investigated the 2009 norovirus outbreak at The Fat Duck claimed the problem might have become worse because Blumenthal had delayed notifying health chiefs. It stated that he first called in private consultants to investigate the outbreak, and only after that did he call the health authorities and local council. In its report on the outbreak, published in the journal *Epidemiology and Infection*, an academic journal published by Cambridge University Press, HPA said: 'Delayed notification of the outbreak to public health authorities may have contributed to outbreak size and duration.' It also claimed that some 66 complaints of illness had been received by Blumenthal's restaurant by the time it contacted the authorities. The report went on to claim that many of the 240 diners who said they were affected by food poisoning might have been spared the infection if The Fat Duck had acted sooner. 'Had the reported illness in diners at the restaurant resulted in the public health authorities being notified earlier, then investigations and appropriate interventions could have taken place sooner, potentially avoiding such a high number of cases over such a long period of time,' it stated.

For Blumenthal and his restaurant this was potentially a public relations nightmare. A strong statement was released giving their side of the story. A spokesman for The Fat Duck began by telling the press that it 'strongly refuted' any accusations of wrongdoing. 'The reported illness in February 2009 at The Fat Duck was confirmed as oysters contaminated at source by norovirus. At the time, we voluntarily closed the restaurant and called in the authorities. We are satisfied with all our procedures that were in place and strongly refute any accusations of wrongdoing.' He went on to add that the restaurant co-operated with all parties 'fully and transparently' and reminded the world that The Fat Duck had received a clean bill of health to re-open after a ten-day investigation. 'We also received full support by our insurers who found no fault in our practices following a report from a leading UK independent specialist.' Moving forward, Blumenthal and his team remain determined to avoid any health issues at work. The restaurant insists that there is still no foolproof safety measure to protect the general public with regards to shellfish and viral contamination. 'For this reason we still do not serve oysters or razor clams at The Fat Duck,' said the spokesman.

* * *

As 2011 came to a close, Blumenthal perhaps deserved a breather following a year of drama. It had been maybe his hardest time since those tough days when he launched his first restaurant. As always, he anticipated Christmas with the excitement of a child. Indeed, the childlike wonder and sense of adventure that remains inside him is what makes him such a fascinating, successful and admirable figure. No wonder he loves Christmas – lots of big kids do. Asked what his plans were, he said, 'I'm going to be in front of a roaring fire, in a rocking chair – I might even put on my favourite bobble hat and my slippers.'

If his needs seem simple, it's because they are. 'I'll be putting my feet up and definitely be having a tipple,' he said.

'Apart from a decent wine with Christmas lunch, the two things I like and only have at Christmas are a glass of sherry, which my great-aunt introduced me to, and a really good malt whisky in front of the fire.' A man often asked for advice on how to create the perfect Christmas dinner experience, he went on to deliver a well-crafted point about the need to enjoy Christmas, and the inherent contradiction in the way some people approach the festive season. 'Christmas Day should be about relaxing and chilling out,' he said. 'If you want lots of people coming around your house, fair enough. But I don't understand why people say, "I've got 38 people coming for Christmas lunch", and get all stressed. If you want that many, then invite them. If you don't want to, don't do it.' It seems a sensible enough tip.

For Blumenthal, meat is not necessarily the pivotal ingredient for a perfect Christmas dinner, though he has amusing memories of the place turkey held during the yuletides of his childhood. 'Growing up, my dad would always get the biggest turkey he could – I think they were the direct descendants of dinosaurs,' he joked. 'But Mum never really liked eating it, so there'd be mountains of leftovers. For me, the best thing about turkey is making those fantastic doorstep sandwiches from the leftovers with loads of mayonnaise. Then of course you are into the turkey curry, turkey bolognese, turkey ice cream. I'm only joking about the turkey ice cream, I've never made that.' The central ingredient of a successful Christmas meal is, he said, the roast potato. 'They are the focal point. You can roast your meat, and let it rest, and you can pre-prepare your veg, but with your roast potatoes – when they're ready, they are ready. I do like to eat them cold if they are left over, but I find that they always go. No matter how many you make, it's very rare that any are left over.'

Looking ahead into 2012, Blumenthal could see an already-busy diary; there were bookings for live appearances in other countries, including Australia. His international commitments complemented a typically busy and ambitious 12 months. We are left with a sense of restlessness; he shows no sign of losing his energy, sense of wonder and love of innovation, despite advancing into middle age. Indeed, far from being 'more of the same' for him, at work and at home Blumenthal is entering new eras in his life. Why should he lose his vigour? Celebrity chefs frequently soar in popularity as they get older: Hugh Fearnley-Whittingstall and Gordon Ramsay are, like Heston, in their forties; Gary Rhodes and Nigella Lawson, their fifties; Rick Stein, his sixties; Delia Smith – amazingly – is in her seventies. All continue to enjoy both their work and enormous love from the public. And historically, famous chefs have continued to be active and enjoy popularity late into life. Fanny Cradock, for instance, was appearing on television in her seventies.

While one should perhaps expect only the unexpected from this eccentric genius, one thing will remain the same for the foreseeable future: the beautiful Berkshire village of Bray will remain the heart of his operation. 'He's got a restaurant in London, but otherwise he's concentrated everything in Bray,' said a spokeswoman. 'That's not going to change. And neither is Bray.' As to what wonders he will conjure up within the walls of his venues, in Bray and the capital, it is a brave writer that would make any predictions. Who but the man himself could have foreseen snail porridge or bacon-and-egg ice cream? It is the fiery ambition and unpredictability of this man that makes him such a fascinating figure. Long may that ambition burn.

ACKNOWLEDGEMENTS

I am grateful to Lucian Randall, John Blake and Rosie Ries. Thanks to Chris Morris, Chris Leonard and Jonathan Sacerdoti. Writing this book was a frequently hunger-provoking experience, so I would like to acknowledge the coffee and food of Bagels and Beans cafe in Amsterdam, which fuelled the writing of several chapters of this book. The chilli and the black pudding at Little Chef Popham were memorable too.

DISCARD

BIBLIOGRAPHY

On Food and Cooking, Harold McGee (James Bennet, 2004)

Kitchen Chemistry, Ted Lister (RSC, 2005)

Family Food, Heston Blumenthal (Penguin, 2002)

In Search of Perfection, Heston Blumenthal (Bloomsbury, 2006)

Further Adventures in Search of Perfection, Heston Blumenthal (Bloomsbury, 2007)

The Big Fat Duck Cookbook, Heston Blumenthal (Bloomsbury, 2008)

In The Kitchen, Monica Ali (Doubleday, 2009)